Praise for *Parenting the Strong-Willed Child*

"I highly recommend *Parenting the Strong-Willed Child* to parents—and to the teachers, psychologists, pediatricians, and other professionals who work with the stressed-out parents of difficult preschoolers. Rex Forehand and Nick Long are nationally recognized authorities who bring their extensive clinical and research experience together in this outstanding book."

— *Robert Emery, Ph.D.*
Professor of Psychology, University of Virginia

"An excellent book for parents. Easy-to-read, but based on solid scientific principles."

— *Andrew Christensen, Ph.D.*
University of California, Los Angeles

"This is a superb rendering of a scientifically proven program for parents of young oppositional children. Parents will find here a wealth of practical advice for managing difficult children. And what is more, it works!"

— *Russell A. Barkley, Ph.D.*
Professor of Psychiatry and Neurology,
University of Massachusetts

"All parents will benefit from the understanding and comprehensive perspective this book provides for how to be a thoughtful, responsible, and effective mother or father."

— *Susan G. O'Leary, Ph.D.*
Professor of Clinical Psychology,
State University of New York at Stonybrook

"A superbly written book offering an exceptionally clear set of recommendations for parents to use in improving their children's behavior and family life."

— *Michael C. Roberts, Ph.D.*
Clinical Child Psychology Program,
University of Kansas

"This is an excellent book written by two renowned researchers who have a wealth of clinical experience as well as firsthand knowledge of what it is to be parents."
—E. Gail Tripp, Ph.D.
Department of Psychology,
University of Otago, Dunedin, New Zealand

"An immensely important addition to any collection of books about parenting."
—Charlotte Johnston, Ph.D.
Associate Professor, Department of Psychology,
University of British Columbia

"As a psychologist and parent of a strong-willed child, I have taught the principles and techniques described in this book to over 200 families and utilized them in my own family with considerable success. What has most impressed me has been in follow-up with families 5 to 10 years after they have completed this parenting program. Parents reported satisfaction with the program, an improved relationship with their child, and fewer occurrences of negative child behavior—a finding confirmed by independent observations of the parent-child interaction!
—Cynthia G. Baum, Ph.D.
Dean, American School of Professional Psychology, Virginia

"The authors have successfully translated complex research theories and findings into a straightforward guide for parents. This guide is true to the scientific backing that it enjoys. Moreover, the authors have written in such a conversational tone that this book is easy to read and to absorb."
—Kenneth A. Dodge, Ph.D.
Professor of Psychology and of Psychiatry,
Vanderbilt University

"This book will be of enormous benefit to the many parents who find themselves doing daily battle with a wilful child. . . . The book reflects the state of art in clinical psychology."
—Mark R. Dadds, Ph.D.
Professor of Psychology & Director of Clinical Training,
Griffith University, Australia

PARENTING
the
strong-willed
child

The Clinically Proven Five-Week Program
for Parents of Two- to Six-Year-Olds

REX FOREHAND, PH.D.,
AND NICHOLAS LONG, PH.D.

CB
CONTEMPORARY BOOKS

Library of Congress Cataloging-in-Publication Data

Forehand, Rex L. (Rex Lloy), 1945–
    Parenting the strong-willed child : the clinically proven five-week
program for parents of two- to six-year-olds / Rex Forehand and
Nicholas Long.
       p.   cm.
    Includes index.
    ISBN 0-8092-3265-0
    1. Problem children—Behavior modification.   2. Child rearing.
3. Parenting.   I. Long, Nicholas, 1956– .   II. Title.
HQ773.F67   1996
649'.64—dc20   95-52118
                                            CIP

Interior design by Terry Stone

Published by Contemporary Books
A division of The McGraw-Hill Companies
4255 West Touhy Avenue, Lincolnwood (Chicago), Illinois 60712-1975 U.S.A.
Printed in the United States of America
International Standard Book Number: 0-8092-3265-0
01 02 03 04 05 06 BR 25 24 23 22 21 20 19 18 17 16 15 14 13 12 11 10 9

This book is dedicated
to the many parents of
strong-willed children.

Contents

Preface

Parenting is one of the most difficult tasks that we, as adults, face. While most of us receive training for our occupations, we enter the world of parenting with little instruction and guidance. As a result, we use mainly trial and error in our attempts to be effective parents. Unfortunately, with a strong-willed child, there is little time for trial and error. You need effective parenting skills, and you need them now!

Perhaps almost as difficult as parenting a strong-willed child is writing a book about how to parent such a child. You have to believe that you know something that can help parents through the difficult times with their strong-willed children. Fortunately, we collectively have spent over thirty years developing and evaluating programs for parents of strong-willed children. From the research data we have systematically collected and the reports of the many parents with whom we have worked, we know that the skills we have taught parents have helped them improve their relationships with their children. These skills have also helped the parents decrease problem behaviors associated with being strong-willed and enabled the children to capitalize on the positive aspects of their strong wills.

Beyond our research and clinical work with parents and their strong-willed children, each of us brings to this book the experience of being a parent. This personal experience is no small part of what appears throughout this book. We know that parenting is not easy under the best of conditions. We know the difficulties of applying the parenting skills taught in this book. We know the highs and lows of parenting. We have experienced it all on a personal level, and this has helped us be realistic in our advice about parenting.

This book could not have been written without the diligent work of many people. Two people in particular stand out. With patience and constant encouragement, Nancy Woodall typed and retyped numerous versions of the manuscript. Corrine David read and reread the text numerous times. These two individuals went substantially beyond the call of duty, and we greatly appreciate their efforts!

We want to express our appreciation to Nancy Crossman at Contemporary Books for the support, encouragement, and feedback she provided. We also want to thank Karen Schenkenfelder, Gigi Grajdura, Maureen Musker, Alina Storek, and the other staff members at Contemporary Books for their valuable contributions.

As you will read throughout this book, the support, love, and learning that come from a family should never be underestimated. This is certainly the case for both authors. The first author (RF) has been fortunate to have experienced support, love, and numerous invaluable learning experiences from his parents, Rex and Sara Forehand, and his children, Laura and Greg Forehand. Thank you! There may be only one person who fell in love in the first grade, never loved anyone else, had the fortune to marry that person, and has been happily married for thirty years. I am that person. Lell, thank you for your support, excitement about life, strength to fight difficulties, ability to laugh at the darkest moment, and, through your need for change, the introduction of new and higher experiences into our lives. But most important, thank you for your love and for being!

The second author (NL) also has been blessed with a loving and supportive family. I would like to thank my parents, John and Jean Long, for providing wonderful examples of what it means to be loving and caring parents. My brother, Adam Long, who was born when I was fifteen years old, helped me realize how wonderful children are and greatly influenced my decision to pursue a career working with children. I want to thank my own children, Justin and Alex Long, for their love and support. I am extremely fortunate to have two such wonderful sons. Finally, I want to thank my wife, Sharon, for being what I consider the best mother in the world. You have taught me so much through your absolute love of being a parent!

It is probably rare for two friends to undertake writing a book together and to have their friendship deepen over the course of the endeavor. However, that is exactly what has happened in our case. There has been mutual inspiration, support, and positive reinforcement. Indeed, we are fortunate to have each other as friends and to have had the opportunity to share this writing experience.

PARENTING
the
strong-willed
child

"The challenges of parenthood are daunting, but its rewards go to the core of what it means to be human—intimacy, growth, learning, and love."

—Carnegie Corporation, 1994

Introduction

Parents of young strong-willed children are frustrated! They are frustrated by their children's behavior as well as the lack of support and resources to help deal with strong-willed children. If you are one of these parents, you are not alone. Most important, there are answers for the negative aspects of your child's strong-willed behavior.

We have spent years developing, evaluating, and using a clinical treatment program that addresses the behavior problems, especially problems of not obeying their parents, often seen in young children who are very strong-willed. We developed this program to help parents of these children. It focuses on teaching parents techniques that they can use to improve their child's behavior.

Over the past twenty years we and many other researchers around the country have studied this clinical program. The research has shown the program to be highly effective. Typical results for families who complete the program include improved parent-child relationships (more positive interactions between parent and child), children who mind their parents more, and fewer child behavior problems at home and in other settings such as preschool. Research that studied children up to fifteen years after completion of this program has found the beneficial results to be lasting.

Because this program is so effective, we have written about it in many professional journals and books. We have also taught the program's parenting techniques to psychologists and other professionals around the country so that they can use the program with the parents with whom they work.

We are committed to helping as many families with a strong-willed child as possible. That is why we decided to write this book for parents. The book covers most of the parenting techniques included in our clinical program. We believe that most parents can learn these clinically proven techniques by reading this book and following its recommendations and exercises. If you use these parenting techniques correctly, they will improve your relationship with your child and reduce many of the problems associated with your child's strong-willed behavior.

While this book is based on our clinical program, it is not a substitute for individual professional help if your child has severe behavior problems or if you are concerned that he might have a disorder such as "hyperactivity." Symptoms of "hyperactivity" (officially know as Attention-Deficit/Hyperactivity Disorder) include *severe* problems with inattention, impulsivity, and high activity. If your child is exhibiting severe problems, we recommend that you consult your child's physician or a mental health professional for evaluation and assistance. However, even for many of the families that need professional guidance, we believe that the techniques presented in this book can still be helpful.

Overview of the Book

Our strategy for addressing strong-willed behavior has three dimensions. The first dimension involves helping you understand your child's strong-willed behavior and how various factors influence such behavior. The second dimension involves teaching specific parenting techniques for addressing the behavior problems most commonly exhibited by strong-willed children two to six years old. The third dimension involves helping you foster a climate within your family and home that will make these parenting techniques most effective. When combined, these three dimensions form a whole strategy you can use to understand your child's behavior and to learn how to change it.

The book is divided into four parts. Each of the first three parts describes a different dimension of our strategy for parenting. The fourth part describes how to combine what you have learned from the previous three parts, along with other practical suggestions, to manage specific behavior problems. Part I explains the factors that cause or contribute to your child's strong-willed behavior. We start by examining the role of temperament in setting the stage for strong-willed behavior. We then address how your reactions to your child's behavior can actually increase your child's strong-willed behavior. We then go on to consider how factors such as parental conflict, divorce, parental mood, alcohol abuse, and television affect a child's behavior.

The parenting techniques in Part II take the form of a five-week program for dealing with the behavior problems associated with being strong-willed. You will learn and practice a new skill every week. By the end of the five weeks, you should notice a significant improvement in your relationship with your child and in your child's behavior.

In Part III we focus on ways to develop a more positive atmosphere in your family and home. The purpose of this part is to enhance and maintain the positive behavior changes that occurred as a result of the five-week program. The chapters in this part explain how you can make your home and family interactions more positive, improve your communication skills, boost your child's self-esteem, and develop greater patience in dealing with your child.

Finally, in Part IV we discuss strategies for managing specific behavior problems commonly reported by parents of young strong-willed children. Each problem is addressed separately, and the recommendations given supplement the parenting skills discussed in Parts II and III.

We hope that this book will help you understand your strong-willed child's behavior, learn effective parenting skills, and learn how to enhance and maintain these parenting skills. We hope that learning how to use these skills, along with other recommendations that we offer to effectively address your major concerns regarding your child's behavior, will, in turn, increase your sense of competency as a parent.

Authors' Note: In referring to children, we decided to use masculine pronouns for ease and clarity, not to imply that girls cannot be as strong-willed as boys. For the same reasons we use primarily feminine pronouns when referring to parents.

PART I

Understanding Your Strong-Willed Child's Behavior

*As parents, we can do a better job of addressing strong
willed behavior if we understand what it is and where it
comes from. If you understand what factors contribute to
your child's behavior, you will be better able to make the
changes necessary to address undesirable behavior. In
Part I we present our views on the role of temperament
in determining your child's behavior (Chapter 1), how
your responses to your child's behavior can actually
increase his strong-willed behavior (Chapter 2), and how
various factors within and outside the family affect your
child's behavior (Chapter 3).*

1

Strong-Willed Behavior and How It All Begins

"He was born with a strong will!" That was what Tommy's parents told us when he was two years old. Several hours after Tommy was born, they said, the hospital nurses started commenting about his temper and how fussy he was. Tommy cried and cried and cried. His parents thought it was colic and that his crying would decrease as he grew older. Unfortunately, as the months passed, the crying and fussing continued. By eighteen months, he was consistently fussing and crying to gain his way or to show he did not like something. He would fuss and cry when he had to sit in his car seat, take a bath, get dressed, go to bed, or do anything else he did not like.

Four-year-old Johnny was very outgoing and independent. Unfortunately, he was also very demanding. His parents and his preschool teacher stated that he was "as stubborn as they come." If he did not get his way, Johnny would become upset and have temper tantrums. These tantrums included yelling, crying, and stamping his feet. Johnny was also very active and intense. He always was on the go and seemingly had boundless energy. As a result of his activity level, he often fell down. Although he rarely hurt himself, he would scream and act as if he had been mortally wounded.

Mary was a six-year-old kindergartner. Testing at school indicated that she had above-average intelligence and academic skills. She was also very confident of her abilities and would persevere in challenging activities long after most other children would give up. However, Mary had never minded her parents very well. This problem with obeying had become worse at home, but not at preschool. Unfortunately, Mary's kindergarten teacher began to have problems with Mary's not complying at school. At first Mary would just ignore instructions her teacher gave her. Then she became openly defiant, saying, "No, I will not do it!" in response to instructions from her teacher. Mary's parents were concerned that, although she was very intelligent, she would be seen by her teachers as a problem child. They were concerned that these perceptions and Mary's behavior would affect her future education.

What Is Strong-Willed Behavior?

The parents of Tommy, Johnny, and Mary all considered their child to be strong-willed. But what does being strong-willed really mean? From our experience, these children usually have a very strong sense of independence. In many ways this is very positive, because individuals who are independent are typically also assertive, confident, determined, and persistent. Unfortunately, a strong sense of independence also frequently leads these young children to become stubborn, argumentative, and defiant. To see whether parents agreed with our view of the characteristics associated with being a "strong-willed child," we conducted a survey. We asked a group of parents of two- to six-year-old children, who were enrolled in a parenting class, to tell us whether or not their child was strong-willed and what they believed were the characteristics of being strong-willed. An amazing 48 percent of the parents reported that their young child was "strong-willed." To read how they described those children, see the box titled "Is Your Child Strong-Willed?"

A strong-willed child can be very frustrating and challenging to a parent (as you probably well know!). Equally important, however, many of their characteristics can be positive ones: persistent, determined, independent, confident, outgoing, questioning, and assertive. *Both positive and negative qualities are associated with being strong-willed.* The key is to nurture your strong-willed child's positive qualities while at the same time minimizing the impact of the negative qualities on himself—and on others.

If you are like most parents of strong-willed children, your child's strong will may continually conflict with what you, as his parent, believe is best for him and your family. If this is the case for you and your child, you will need to work with him to direct his strong will in more appropriate ways. The purpose of this book is to help you do this by decreasing the negative aspects of your child's strong will while encouraging him to use his strong will in positive ways. We hope that your child will learn to use his strong will to excel in life.

In the Beginning There Was Temperament

How does a child become strong-willed? Many of the characteristics of being strong-willed have their roots in a child's temperament. As you will read in Chapters 2 and 3, a child's temperament interacts with a number of factors, particularly parenting, to determine the behavior

Is Your Child Strong-Willed?

If your child is strong-willed, you probably have known it since he was a baby! These are the children who feel their wants and needs strongly, and they rarely hesitate to let you know just how they feel. A group of parents in a parenting class described their own strong-willed children in the following terms:

- "If she doesn't want to do something, there is no way you can make her do it"
- "Always wanting to do everything for herself"
- "Demands constant attention"
- "Always wanting to make the decisions/choices"
- "Not recognizing authority of adults/parents"
- "Persistent"
- "Unpredictable"
- "Stubborn"
- "Independent"
- "Determined"
- "Temperamental"
- "Bad temper"
- "Talks back a lot"
- "Overly sensitive"
- "Frequent temper tantrums"
- "Negative reactions— everything is a fight or a struggle"
- "Won't mind"
- "Resists direction"
- "Doesn't respond to discipline"
- "Knows no limits"
- "Tells us what to do"
- "Very outgoing"
- "Resists anything done to him—diaper changes, bath, dressing, etc."
- "Headstrong"
- "Argumentative"
- "Aggressive"
- "Often upset"
- "Dominant"
- "Confident"
- "Questioning"
- "Assertive"
- "Goes out of her way to complete a task even if you show an easier way the task can be completed"
- "Cries to get her way constantly"
- "Her way or no way—no matter what"
- "Argues every point"
- "Pushes things to the extreme"
- "Works on a frustrating task (maybe one that is over his age level) until completed"
- "Will focus on one thing and be persistent until she gets what she wants"
- "Has own ideas"
- "Resistant to change"

Do any of these descriptions sound like your child? If so, you have a lot of company!

that can be labeled strong-willed. This chapter will focus on helping you understand temperament and its relationship to the behavior of children and their parents.

Temperament generally refers to a child's inborn behavioral style or innate tendencies to act a certain way. Temperament is reflected in how a child typically approaches, interacts in, and experiences social relationships. Imagine two fifteen-month-old children who fall down while running across a lawn. Neither child is injured, but one child starts to scream and cry following the fall. The other child laughs after he falls, gets up, and starts to run again. The different ways these children handled the fall reflect, in part, their temperaments.

Temperament is generally considered to be inborn. Many professionals believe that a child's basic temperament can be observed in early infancy, well before a particular parenting style has had time to have a major impact on his behavior. However, as we will show you later, your child's actual behavior (for example, what he does when told "no") is a function of both his temperament and your parenting.

Researchers have identified numerous temperament traits. A child's overall temperament is the combination of these individual traits. While there is not a pure "strong-willed temperament," there are several temperament traits that are easily observed in many strong-willed children. These temperament traits include reactivity, adaptability, persistence, and emotionality. Let us briefly describe each of these traits and how each is associated with being strong-willed.

Reactivity refers to how intensely a child reacts, either positively or negatively, to different situations or events. For example, a child may respond in different ways to being told "no" by his mother. In our experience, strong-willed children are typically quite intense in their reactions. When they react, you know it! Thus, a strong-willed child may scream, cry, and even hit in response to being told "no."

Adaptability refers to how well a child adapts to

changes in situations and events. Strong-willed children often have a difficult time adapting to transitions. Transitions that are particularly difficult for strong-willed children involve stopping a fun activity or having to start something they do not really want to do.

Persistence refers to how long a child stays with an activity. Strong-willed children are typically quite persistent. Persistence is often displayed in positive ways, such as persevering with challenging activities. However, strong-willed children are often also persistent in negative ways such as being stubborn and demanding.

Emotionality refers to stability and the positive/negative aspects of a child's mood or emotions. In our experience, strong-willed children tend to have inconsistent moods. For example, they will frequently shift between having good days and having bad days. Unfortunately, many strong-willed children tend to have more bad days than good days. That is, they are often fussy and moody. It is important to remember that this fussiness and moodiness usually reflects a temperamental trait or behavioral style.

In summary, there are several specific temperament traits that we frequently observe in strong-willed children. This observation leads to the next question: are these early temperament traits associated with later behavior problems?

According to a number of research studies, a child's early temperament is significantly related to his later behavior. For example, toddlers who have trouble adapting to new situations and who are generally quick to overreact tend to have more behavior problems in the preschool years. A child's early temperament has been linked not only to later behavior problems but also to later issues related to peer relationships, preschool adjustment, and even academic achievement. (However, as we will discuss next, most of these same studies indicate that temperament cannot explain the whole story about the behavior of a child.)

Temperament, Parenting, and Behavior

Temperament and parenting style both determine your child's behavior. Many parents ask us whether it is their child's temperament or their parenting that has "caused" their child's strong-willed behavior. Such a question is a variation of the often-debated question of whether "nature" or "nurture" is most important in determining our personality. Since temperament and parenting continually interact, we seldom can know which is *more* important in determining a child's strong-willed behavior.

What is clear is that temperament and parenting are both important and inextricably linked. Recent research suggests that many of the temperament traits we have been discussing can change as a child develops. That is, many of these temperament traits are not "biologically fixed" but rather are tendencies that can be modified by parenting style and other environmental factors. As we will discuss in Chapter 2, we believe that strong-willed children typically have certain temperamental traits or tendencies that evoke certain parenting practices. These practices, in turn, often strengthen the very strong willed behaviors that parents want to decrease. This is good news, since it means your strong-willed child's behavior is not biologically predestined by his temperament! You can influence your child's behavior through your parenting practices.

In summary, strong-willed behavior is common among young children and often has its roots in a child's early temperament. However, you *can* change the negative aspects of your child's strong-willed behavior through your parenting. In fact, that is probably why you bought this book!

2

Why Is My Child Becoming Even More Strong-Willed?

The evidence suggests that many children are born with a strong-willed disposition, and this is not necessarily good or bad. However, a young strong-willed child may engage in more and more of the negative behaviors we associate with a strong will—stubbornness, impatience, tantrums, and so on. In that case, strong-willed behavior becomes a problem. And a key factor that determines whether the child's behavior becomes problematic is the way the parents manage the behavior.

If your child's behavior is becoming worse, don't simply blame yourself, however. The way you have been responding to your child's behavior has been, in part, a function of his behavior. Unfortunately, strong-willed children often bring out the worst in parents. Responding appropriately to a child with an easy temperament is relatively easy. In contrast, when faced with the frustrations of managing a strong-willed child, parents are much more likely to yell or use other less-than-ideal parenting strategies.

In this chapter we discuss how your child's behavior affects the way you respond to it and how your response affects his behavior. We will start by summarizing ways children learn to behave through their interactions with others. Our goal in this chapter is to provide you with a basic understanding of how a child's behavior develops as a result of the environment in which he lives. This will help you analyze and solve the problem behaviors of your strong-willed child.

Learning Through Social Interactions

Much of how a child behaves is learned from interactions with others. Temperament and other factors lay the groundwork, but it is through social learning that children establish most specific behaviors, both appropriate and inappropriate. Social learning occurs in three major ways: through modeling, reinforcement, and punishment.

Modeling

Modeling is basically learning by example. It occurs when a child learns how to behave a certain way by observing others behaving that way. Your child may observe another child having a tantrum because the child wants a cookie. If the child receives the cookie after the tantrum, your child learns, by observation, that a tantrum may be an effective way to get something. The next time your child wants something, he is more likely to have a tantrum.

Observing someone behave in a certain way does not mean your child will automatically behave that way, but it does increase the chances that he might. Whether your child will imitate someone depends on many things, including whether he wants to be like that other person, how many times he observes the behavior, and whether the behavior observed had a positive outcome (like the child receiving the cookie to stop the tantrum).

Modeling is a very important and powerful learning mechanism. You need to make sure that the behavior you "model" for your child is appropriate. Since young children look up to their parents, they are especially likely to behave like their parents as a result of modeling. For example, losing your temper in front of your child when you become frustrated increases the chance that your child will handle frustration in a similar fashion. Children often look to their parents for examples of how to behave in difficult situations. The philosophy "Do as I say, not as I do" does not work because modeling is more powerful than words in teaching children how to behave. Set a good example for your child! If you are strong-willed yourself, try to model the positive behaviors associated with being strong-willed, not the negative behaviors. For example, when you are upset with someone, try to model appropriate assertiveness, not aggressiveness. Also, model persistence when you face challenging tasks. Let your child see you keep doing something difficult until you are successful.

Reinforcement

When most people think of *reinforcement*, they tend to think of giving children things like candy or money in exchange for good behavior. Such an understanding of reinforcement is immensely oversimplified and does not do the principle of reinforcement justice. Although many people resist the notion, reinforcement guides much of our behavior. In fact, it is a major key to the development of our social skills. The principle of reinforcement is simply that if a behavior is followed by something positive, the behavior is strengthened and is more likely to occur in the future.

We are not saying a child's social behavior is primarily guided by someone giving him material things whenever he behaves in certain ways. Most reinforcers are *social* in nature. These social reinforcers—attention, smiles, laughter, and so on—have the greatest impact on your behavior and on your child's behavior. Much of your child's behavior is gradually established through social reinforcers that occur over and over again each day. No single reinforcer will have a dramatic impact on behavior. Reinforcers work slowly and have to occur repeatedly in order to significantly change a person's behavior.

Think about situations in your life where social reinforcers guide your behavior. For example, you are more likely to talk to someone who smiles at you as you approach than to someone who looks away. This is usually because your past experiences have been positive (reinforced) when you talked to individuals who smiled at you. Similarly, you probably spend more time talking to someone who gives you attention and makes you laugh. Your talking is being reinforced by the attention and laughing. In the same way, your child is reinforced more by little but frequent responses to him, such as a touch, a smile, a compliment, a positive glance, or a word of encouragement, than by material rewards such as toys, candy, or money. (And a parent who gives a lot of reinforcement to her child tends to receive a lot of reinforcement from her child in return.) One mother who went through our clinical program told us, "When I started smiling more at my child, he started to smile more at me. It made me feel so good."

Another kind of reinforcement is *negative reinforcement*. Many people confuse negative reinforcement and punishment, but they are not the same. Negative reinforcement, like positive reinforcement, strengthens behavior. However, in negative reinforcement, a behavior is reinforced not because it results in something positive, but because it results in the removal or end of something negative. Suppose your child is playing in a sandbox and another child is constantly throwing sand, which blows into your child's face. Your child goes over to the other child and assertively says, "Stop throwing the sand." If the other child stops throwing the sand, your child's assertiveness will have been negatively reinforced. That is, your child's assertiveness was followed not by something positive being given but by the end of something negative (blowing sand). Your child's assertiveness is strengthened, and he is more likely to be assertive in the future. Negative reinforcement can be difficult to fully understand, but it is important. It can play a major role in the development of disruptive behavior, as we will discuss later in this chapter.

Punishment

Whereas reinforcement strengthens behavior, *punishment* weakens behavior. In the minds of many parents, punishment means spanking. However, spanking is only one type of punishment. Punishment includes time-outs, reprimands, removal of privileges, and anything else that follows a behavior and weakens it.

Although a single punishment rarely leads to any long-term changes in behavior, punishment can be effective if used appropriately and consistently. However, relying too much on punishment to change your child's behavior can lead to problems such as these:

- Punishment gives a child the message of what not to do, without necessarily teaching what to do.
- To maintain the effectiveness of punishment, parents often have to use increasingly harsher punishment. If punishment becomes significantly more frequent and intense over time, it can lead to problems such as child abuse.
- Frequent punishment can lead your child to start disliking you, resenting you, and becoming aggressive toward you.
- Individuals who give a lot of punishment tend to receive a lot of punishment in return. As with reinforcement, you tend to receive what you give. For example, parents who use excessive punishment frequently find themselves on the receiving end of their child's indignation.

In summary, using some types of punishment, such as time-out, sparingly and within a framework of a lot of reinforcement can be effective. However, excessive use of punishment may create more problems than it solves.

Accidentally Reinforcing Your Child's Inappropriate Behavior

Although much of your child's social learning takes place through reinforcement, parents often provide the reinforcement without being aware of it. The reinforcement occurs naturally within everyday interactions. Unfortunately, we often end up reinforcing the exact behaviors we are trying to eliminate.

Sometimes a parent inadvertently rewards her child's inappropriate behavior. For example, when you are shopping with your child, he may see a toy he wants. He starts to cry and whine. You try to comfort and calm him. Still whining and crying, he asks you again for the toy. You hate to see him upset, so you agree to buy the toy for him. What has happened in this interaction? You rewarded your child for crying and fussing by providing attention and comfort as well as by purchasing the toy. What has your child learned? He has learned that he can sometimes get your attention and his own way by crying and fussing. The next time he wants something, he is more likely to cry and whine in an effort to receive what he wants. We call this the *positive reinforcement trap*.

A single incident like the example above will not permanently affect your child's behavior. However, when this type of interaction occurs repeatedly, it can lead to a significant escalation of crying, fussing, or other inappropriate behaviors. Since you surely don't want to reward your child's inappropriate behavior, analyze your behavior. Are you unintentionally rewarding your child's inappropriate behavior? If so, try to stop. If you find it extremely difficult to stop, do not be surprised. Old habits are hard to change. The parenting program presented in Part II will help you escape the positive reinforcement trap.

Children also learn to misbehave in order to avoid something they do not like. For example, you tell your child to pick up the toys that he has left on the floor. He does not pick them up, so you start reminding him over and over. Out of frustration, you resort to nagging. As you are nagging him, he turns to you, starts to cry, and calls you "mean" as he runs to his room. You decide that it's just not worth the frustration to make him pick up the toys. You pick up the toys and put them away. What happened in this situation? Well, your child learned that by crying, calling you a name, and running away from you, he made you stop the nagging, and he did not have to pick up the toys. This is an example of the *negative reinforce ment trap*.

Just as with the positive reinforcement trap, a single incident involving negative reinforcement will not permanently affect your child's behavior. However, when this type of interaction occurs repeatedly, it can lead to a significant escalation in crying, fussing, or other inappropriate behaviors.

The Coercive Process

A negative reinforcement trap rarely occurs in isolation. Complex interactions between a parent and child often involve both individuals falling into the negative reinforcement trap. Gerald Patterson, an internationally renowned researcher at the Oregon Social Learning Center, has studied this phenomenon extensively and has identified what he calls the "coercive process." This process occurs in many families with a young child who is strong-willed. When the coercive process occurs repeatedly during the hundreds of interactions between a parent and child each week, a child's behavior and the parent's man-

Are You Rewarding the Behaviors You Don't Like?

In spite of our best intentions as parents, we often reinforce the very behaviors we most want to end. Have you ever responded to your child's behavior in any of the following ways?

- Repeatedly responding to your child's calls after he has gone to bed
- Comforting your child when he has a tantrum
- Giving attention to your child each time he interrupts your conversation with another adult
- Laughing at your child's inappropriate behavior
- Giving your child candy in the grocery store when he starts crying
- Letting your child sleep with you every night just because he begs to do so

If you have done these things, you have fallen into the positive reinforcement trap. You are encouraging the inappropriate behavior by rewarding it with attention, comfort, laughter, and so on.

Many parents also fall prey to the negative reinforcement trap. Do any of these actions sound familiar?

- Letting your child skip his bath because he cries when you say "bathtime"
- Telling your child to get out of the bathtub but, because he cries, letting him stay in longer
- Letting your child leave an event because he begs not to stay and has a tantrum
- Canceling the baby-sitter because your child cries when you tell him you are going out
- Telling your child to sit quietly at the dinner table but, because he has a tantrum, letting him leave the table
- Taking your child out of his car seat because he cries to get out

These responses to negative behavior reinforce the behavior by ending something your child perceived as unpleasant, be it taking a bath, sitting at the dinner table, or spending an evening with a baby-sitter.

Fortunately, there is an escape from both of these traps. The details are in Part II.

agement of the behavior gradually become more and more negative as each person's behavior receives frequent negative reinforcement.

As an example of the coercive process, imagine you take your child to a store and tell him to hold your hand. He does not want to hold your hand, so he starts whining and trying to pull away to escape your clutch. Out of frustration, you eventually give up and let go of his hand so that you do not have to deal with his fussiness and constant tugging. In this situation, his fussing and resistance to your direction to hold your hand were negatively reinforced by your giving in to him. But your giving in also was negatively reinforced because it stopped his fussing and resistance. As a result of this interaction, your child will more likely resist you and fuss to get his way in the future, and you will more likely give in to his resistance and fussiness because, by giving in, you stopped the problems in the short run.

Now let's add a different twist to the same example. In this case, when your child whines and physically resists holding your hand, you raise your voice and tell him that he has to hold your hand. The resistance continues and, in fact, becomes worse. You lose your temper and start yelling at him. He stops resisting. In this case your yelling was negatively reinforced because it stopped the resistance. This will increase the chances of your yelling at him again in the future.

The problem is that, through the coercive processes described above, a child's behavior gradually becomes more negative and a parent's response to the negative behavior gradually becomes more and more aversive. For example, your child's temper tantrums or other negative behaviors might become more intense and frequent, while at the same time you start to yell or spank more intensely and frequently. This downward cycle will continue as you are each occasionally reinforced for use of increasingly negative behavior. How are you reinforced? By the termination of the other person's negative behavior. One more

The Coercive Process

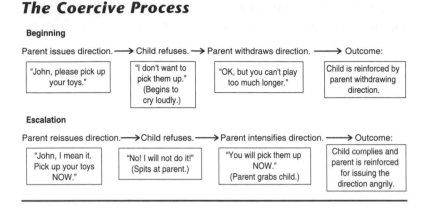

Beginning

Parent issues direction. ⟶ Child refuses. ⟶ Parent withdraws direction. ⟶ Outcome:

| "John, please pick up your toys." | "I don't want to pick them up." (Begins to cry loudly.) | "OK, but you can't play too much longer." | Child is reinforced by parent withdrawing direction. |

Escalation

Parent reissues direction. ⟶ Child refuses. ⟶ Parent intensifies direction. ⟶ Outcome:

| "John, I mean it. Pick up your toys NOW." | "No! I will not do it!" (Spits at parent.) | "You will pick them up NOW." (Parent grabs child.) | Child complies and parent is reinforced for issuing the direction angrily. |

example of the coercive process is presented in the figure at the top of this page. The child's behavior illustrated in the figure—failure to follow directions—is common among strong-willed children.

The coercive process is difficult to grasp. But even if you do not completely understand it, we hope you can appreciate that the way you manage your child's behavior can play a significant role in the development of later problems. The way you behave influences his behavior now—and also the way you will manage his behavior in the future. This effect occurs not as a result of isolated incidents, but through an ongoing series of complex interactions between a parent and child.

Other Factors That Contribute to Strong-Willed Behavior Problems

Besides the positive reinforcement trap and the negative reinforcement trap (which escalates in the coercive process), several other factors may lead to your child becoming increasingly strong-willed. Parents who have children with behavior problems tend to pay less attention to their children's positive behaviors. This typically occurs because these parents become so frustrated in having to deal with their child's negative behaviors that they have a hard time noticing and acknowledging the behaviors that are positive. As the parent of a strong-willed child, you need to make an extra effort to acknowledge and praise your child's positive behaviors. Make sure you let your child know that you notice the times he does do what you tell him. We will discuss this issue in greater detail in Parts II and III.

Parents of strong-willed children also are often uncertain how to manage their child's disruptive behavior. This uncertainty can result in an inconsistent pattern of discipline. A parent who feels overwhelmed and questions her ability to manage her child's disruptive behavior may withdraw from the situation and not intervene at all. At other times she may become frustrated and resort to overly aggressive ways of managing her child's disruptive behavior—for example, losing her temper and yelling or spanking excessively. Neither an overly permissive nor an aggressive parenting style is very effective. In fact, these styles tend to escalate behavior problems, especially when used inconsistently. The five-week parenting program presented in Part II can help you become a more positive and consistent parent.

Modeling is one of the most powerful forms of teaching both positive and negative behaviors. If your strong-willed child is frequently around other children who often misbehave, he may start to copy their negative behaviors. This will be especially true if your child does not observe an adult effectively managing the other children's misbehavior. Take charge and create an environment that is positive for your child. Arrange play situations with friends that do not feed into your child's negative behavior. Try to encourage him to interact with children who are generally well behaved. Just like bad behavior, good behavior will rub off!

Children also model the behavior of their parents, as we discussed earlier in this chapter. If you frequently yell when frustrated, your child will learn to yell when he becomes frustrated. If you hit when angry, your child will learn to hit when he becomes angry. On the positive side, if you model appropriate behavior, your child likely will behave more appropriately. When you become frustrated or angry, try to stay calm and model appropriate ways of handling the situation. The important point is to remember to set a good example for your child.

The negative behaviors we associate with being strong-willed may become more pronounced if your child does not get enough sleep. Tired children often are fussy. The fussiness, in turn, can trigger the negative interactions associated with the coercive process. As a result, the fussiness may contribute to their behavior problems as the parent and child become increasingly negative with one another. If your child is not getting enough sleep, there are several things that you can do. For some suggestions, see Part IV.

If your child seems to be engaging in more and more negative behaviors associated with having a strong will, Table 2-1 may help. It summarizes the reasons for becoming increasingly strong-willed that we described in this chapter. Might some of these reasons apply to you and your child? If so, this book has many ideas to improve your parenting skills and your child's behavior.

Reasons Children Become Increasingly Strong-Willed	TABLE 2-1

- Positive reinforcement trap
- Negative reinforcement trap
- Coercive process (repeated negative reinforcement traps set by parent and child)
- Little attention to positive behavior
- Inconsistency in responding to behavior problems
- Peer modeling of inappropriate behavior
- Parental modeling of inappropriate behavior
- Lack of adequate rest

3

There Is More than Just Good Parenting

Good parenting skills alone cannot guarantee that your child will always behave as you wish. Besides your child's temperament and your parenting techniques, many other things can influence your child's behavior. Among the most important are problems that put stress on families and influences that come from outside the family. In this chapter, we will examine how six sources of family stress—divorce, remarriage, conflict, depressed mood, physical illness, or alcohol abuse—can affect parenting and children's behavior. The figure on the next page presents a model showing that each of these circumstances, and others, can constitute a source of stress that can directly or indirectly, through parenting, affect children's behavior. We also will consider two outside influences on your child's behavior: television, and peer pressure (also shown in the figure). The six sources of family stress, television viewing, and peers can have negative effects on your child, but you have some ability to limit or modify those effects. This chapter will explain how.

Family Stress, Parenting, and Your Child's Behavior

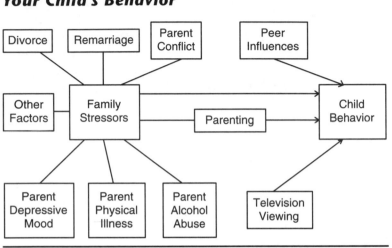

Of course, many other stressors, including economic hardship, work problems, and abuse of drugs (other than alcohol), also can be family stressors. We focus on six of the most important stressors to give you a broad understanding of how such stressors can affect children. We selected these six stressors and two outside influences because ample research has examined their impact on children.

Divorce

Every year over a million children experience parental divorce in the United States. Based on current divorce trends, about 30 percent of children born in the 1990s will experience a parental divorce before they reach the age of eighteen. Divorce and single-parent families have become a way of life in our society.

Research indicates that divorce can have a negative impact on the behavior of children; however, this impact is not nearly as great as the public media often report. Also, some evidence suggests that the behavior of preschool children improves over the two years following divorce. Most important, many of the problems children experience following parental divorce are not due simply to the separation of their parents. Children's adjustment following parental divorce depends, to a large extent, on the situation existing after the divorce. Fortunately, you as a parent often can control many aspects of the situation that may affect your child's adjustment.

If you and your spouse decide to divorce, the first way to help your child adjust is to find a constructive way to explain the divorce to him. The box titled "Telling Your Child About Your Divorce" provides guidelines for doing this. Then, after a separation and divorce, there are many other things you can do to enhance your child's adjustment to this family disruption:

- *Subject your child to as few changes as possible as a result of the divorce.* Try to have your child attend the same preschool or school, continue to live in the same home, and so on. Of particular importance is consistency in your child's standard of living. For this reason, regular child support payments are often critical.
- *Maintain a good relationship with your child.* Spend time talking and doing fun activities together. A good relationship between you and your child can help protect him from many of the stresses of divorce.
- *Consistent discipline is important.* Both parents should use similar, age-appropriate discipline techniques. Limits on what is and is not acceptable behavior for your child also should be consistent between the two homes.
- *Have a consistent pattern of frequent visits with the non-custodial parent.* Frequent cancellations, long periods of no contact, and sporadic visitation schedules may harm your child.
- *Separate spouse and parent roles.* You should work hard to separate your feelings and actions toward your ex-spouse as a partner and lover from those you have

Telling Your Child About Your Divorce

A divorce is a painful process even if no children are involved. And when there are, parents must face the challenge of telling their children what is happening. If you are going through a divorce (or planning to do so), prepare your child as constructively as possible:

- *Jointly decide about telling your child.* You and your spouse need to meet and decide how and when to tell your child. All family members need to hear the same information at the same time.
- *Tell your child.* You want your child to hear about the divorce from you, not from someone else.
- *Be honest and straightforward.* Presenting the truth on a level appropriate for your child will be best for him.
- *Explain exactly what is going to happen.* Tell your child that Mom and Dad are not going to live together anymore. Tell him when specific changes are going to happen.
- *Tell your child about potential changes.* These include with whom he will live and whether he will move, change schools, and keep his pets. Let him know if he will continue to see all grandparents, aunts, uncles, and cousins regularly.
- *Tell him both parents will continue to love him.* Your child needs to hear that your divorce does not change your or his other parent's love for him.
- *Clear your child of guilt.* Preschool children sometimes believe that the reason for the divorce is something they did or did not do. Be clear with your child that this is not the case.
- *Do not assess blame.* Which parent is to blame for the divorce should not be a concern of your child.
- *Encourage questions.* You can prevent your child from having misconceptions by encouraging him to ask questions when you tell him about the divorce and anytime afterward.
- *Repeat information.* Your preschool child may not fully comprehend the information or its meaning for him. You need to plan several occasions to go over the information with him.

about him as a parent. Do not punish your ex-spouse for things he did as a partner and lover by denying him the right to continue being a parent.

- *Do not argue or fight with your ex-spouse in your child's presence.* The amount of parental conflict (over visitation, support, and so on) that your child witnesses following divorce often is directly related to how many problem behaviors he has.
- *Do not use your child as a messenger in parental communications.* Your child should never be asked to communicate messages such as "Tell your dad that he is late with the child support payment."
- *Do not use your child as a spy.* You should not ask your child questions about your ex-spouse's life (such as questions about whom he is dating).
- *Do not use your child as an ally in parental battles.* Avoid bringing your child into battles with your ex-spouse.
- *Do not criticize your ex-spouse in front of your child.* Remember that your ex-spouse (no matter how much anger you feel toward him) is still your child's parent. Whenever possible, it is important for your child to have a loving relationship with both parents.
- *Do not burden your child with personal fears and concerns.* Do not turn to your child for support. Children have enough difficulty making their own adjustment without the added burden of your problems.

Following these guidelines will help minimize the negative effects of divorce on your child.

Remarriage

Most parents who divorce will remarry in the next five years. Like divorce, remarriage is becoming a way of life in American society. Remarriage places parents in a challenging situation. You have to develop the new marriage within the context of the relationship you have with your child and your ex-spouse. Also, your new spouse will bring into the marriage his kinships, possibly including his children. You have to form workable relationships with these people. Finally, you need to help define and develop the parenting role to be played by the new spouse.

When children are in the physical custody of their mother, the effects of her remarriage differ for sons and daughters. Boys' behavior generally appears to improve somewhat compared with that of boys living with a mother who has not remarried. Some authorities believe this is because remarriage brings a male figure and role model back into the home. For girls, the situation appears to be the reverse; they typically do somewhat less well in remarried families than in divorced families. Some authorities believe this occurs because girls may lose the closeness of the relationship they developed with their mothers before remarriage. However, these reactions to remarriage reflect general tendencies and are not true for all children.

As with divorce, the remarriage itself is often less important to the child than how the parents handle the situation. Many of the guidelines for telling your child about your divorce apply to telling him about your new marriage. You can also help your child adjust to this family change in the following ways:

- *Subject your child to as few changes as possible.* If you can, stay in the same community so that he can keep his friends and continue in the same preschool or school. Having a new person become a member of the family will be enough change.
- *Maintain a good relationship with your child.* Do not make your child feel as if he has been replaced by your new spouse. Spend extra time talking with your child. Schedule fun activities that just the two of you do.
- *Explain to your child the parental roles of your new spouse and your ex-spouse.* These roles need to be worked out (obviously, this is no easy task!) and communicated to your child. Your new spouse typically should not

attempt to take over and change the parenting authority in the family but instead should be supportive of
your parenting.

- *Do not let your child divide you and your new spouse.* A
  strong-willed child is just that—strong-willed. He may
  not like a new parent in the home, and he may do
  whatever he can to create tension in your new marriage.
  Stick together and keep channels of communication
  open.
- *Be patient.* It will take time, love, and good parenting!

Parental Conflict

Continued parental conflict in front of your child is more
harmful for him than divorce! That doesn't mean you and
your spouse should divorce rather than have occasional
conflict or that you should never disagree in front of your
child. Resolving disagreements in a constructive way may
actually serve as an example to him about how to deal
with differences of opinion. However, if you and your
spouse have frequent hostile conflicts in front of your
child, you are modeling inappropriate ways to address
differences. Furthermore, your child may feel anxious
about what the conflict means (thinking, for example,
"My parents hate each other and are going to divorce").
Frequent hostile arguments may also disrupt your ability
to parent effectively. Here are some ways to minimize the
negative effects of parental conflict on your child:

- *Do not argue in front of your child.* All parents have disagreements; however, major disagreements should not
  occur in front of your child.
- *Support each other in parenting practices.* Do not let your
  conflict spill over into or disrupt your parenting. Whatever your source of conflict, work together in parenting.
- *Make the best of conflict that does occur in front of your
  child.* Model good communication and conflict resolution skills to reach a solution (see Chapter 12). Explain

to your child the source of the conflict, why you and your spouse disagree, and that he should not side with either parent.

- *Maintain a good relationship with your child.* If both of you as parents work on your relationship with your child, his feelings of insecurity over the conflict and its meaning will be reduced. As in the case of divorce, do not use your child as a messenger, spy, or ally; do not criticize your spouse to your child; and do not burden your child with your fears and concerns.

Depressive Mood

Clinical depression is more than being in a gloomy mood. But even if you just have the blues, your mood can have a negative impact on your child. Your mood can influence how you perceive his behavior, how you parent, and how he behaves. When you feel down, you may be less understanding and tolerant of your child, so you overreact to his problem behaviors. You then may feel even worse and withdraw from your child, or you may feel guilty and become more lax for a while. Once your mood improves, you may interact more consistently in a positive way with him and enforce rules you have established. In short, as your mood goes up and down, your parenting practices change, which is confusing for your child.

If you are a person whose mood often changes, the following guidelines will help minimize the effects on your child:

- *Evaluate your moods.* Do they change frequently? Do you often respond to your child based on your mood? If so, try to develop a positive and consistent mood yourself or seek outside professional help.
- *Monitor your moods.* Note what occurs before and during mood change. This can help you identify what influences your moods and may help you address issues related to your moods.

- *Rely on your spouse for co-parenting.* Your spouse can help compensate for parenting difficulties you experience because of your depressive moods. He can work on maintaining a good relationship with your child and using good parenting skills.
- *Tell your spouse and child when you are feeling down.* Do not expect them to "read your mood." Tell them and solicit their help in making it through the day.
- *Work toward consistent parenting.* If you have clear guidelines for yourself as a parent, like those in our five-week program (Chapters 4–9), your parenting will be less influenced by your mood.

Physical Illness

You or your spouse almost certainly will experience a physical illness at some time. The exact consequences to your family will depend on many variables, including whether the onset of the illness is sudden vs. gradual, the degree to which you are incapacitated, and the course and outcome of the illness. In general, however, a physical illness can deplete your energy, tolerance, and patience for dealing with your child. In some cases, it may even physically limit your parenting abilities.

To minimize the effects of your physical illness on your child, follow these guidelines:

- *Educate yourself about your illness.* You cannot understand your illness unless you educate yourself. In most cases, no one will do it for you.
- *Evaluate your illness.* Examine its dimensions and how it affects your parenting.
- *Monitor your illness.* This can help you identify conditions that positively and adversely influence it.
- *Tell your child about your illness.* Be straightforward and honest. For most illnesses, you should tell him the name of the illness, how it makes you feel, how it is treated, how long you may be ill, and the mostly likely outcome. Give him as much hope as you can.

- *Explain your child's role in the illness.* Assure him that he is *not* responsible in any way for your illness.
- *Explain to him how the family will run while you are ill.* If you usually do certain things (such as cooking meals), explain who will take over these responsibilities. Give your child some new age-appropriate responsibilities so that he will feel he is helping out.
- *Tell your spouse and child when your illness is better and worse.* They need to know how you are doing. Do not expect them to automatically know.
- *Rely on your spouse for co-parenting.* Your spouse can help compensate for parenting difficulties you experience.
- *Let other family members help.* Have other family members and friends help with routine activities (cooking, cleaning, shopping, and so on), so your spouse can spend more time with your child.
- *Work toward consistent parenting.* If you have realistic and clear guidelines for yourself as a parent, your parenting will be less influenced by your illness.

Alcohol Abuse

Use of alcohol by adults is a well-established and generally accepted part of our society. Most people who choose to drink use alcohol on social occasions and for relaxation. However, the abuse of alcohol through excessive drinking can interfere with good parenting. Such drinking can lead you to be inconsistent and less positive in your interactions with your child, to perceive your child's behavior more negatively than it actually is, and to use excessively harsh discipline. Furthermore, many of the behaviors you model for your child when you abuse alcohol, including the excessive drinking itself, are not ones you want your child to emulate. Parents who turn to drinking as an escape from the problem behaviors of their strong-willed child find that it does not work—the strong-willed behavior is still there when they sober up.

If you drink, you need to consider how this affects you as a parent. The following practices and principles will help you address the influence of your drinking on your child and reduce negative effects:

- *Evaluate your drinking patterns.* When, how much, and how often do you drink? Does it interfere with your parenting? If so, change your drinking patterns yourself or seek professional help.
- *Monitor your drinking patterns.* Keep a record of when you drink more and less and what is happening during these times. This can help you identify what conditions are associated with increases and decreases in drinking and whether your drinking interferes with parenting.
- *Rely on your spouse's opinion about your drinking patterns.* Those who drink excessively are rarely good judges of their own drinking.
- *Work toward consistent parenting.* If you have clear guidelines for yourself as a parent, your parenting will be less influenced by your drinking.
- *Don't drink and discipline!* If you drink, do not try to discipline your child. Have your spouse or someone else assume disciplining responsibilities during this time.

Television Viewing

In the past fifty years, television has become an important part of most children's lives. Sadly, at the present time, children in the United States spend more time watching television than they do in any other activity except sleeping. Television can have both negative and positive effects on children. The violence, sex, and advertisements for alcohol use are clearly negative. Many programs imply that power, prestige, and physical attractiveness are the most important personal qualities to strive for. Characters are often not held accountable for their actions. Also, watching a lot of television is associated with obesity, less

Children and Television Viewing

Many people fail to realize the impact television has on the lives of our children. Consider these facts:

- Children ages two to eleven watch an average of about twenty-eight hours of television per week!
- The amount of television watching by children has steadily increased over the past thirty years.
- Only 5 to 25 percent of the average child's television viewing is of programs specifically produced for children.
- Approximately 30 percent of preschoolers are allowed to watch television whenever they want.
- By age eighteen, the average child has seen over eighteen thousand murders on television.
- Children who watch the most television tend to have the lowest grades at school.
- Children who read well tend to watch less television.

creativity, and less interaction with family and friends. In other words, it isn't always what your child is watching but what he *isn't doing* that may be most harmful. On the other hand, there are some wonderful television programs that promote learning and growth. Many educational programs teach important skills such as spelling and reading.

Parents can do many things to minimize the negative effects of television. At the same time, parents can encourage their children to use television as a tool for learning. These suggestions for television viewing include both kinds of responses:

- *Encourage viewing of programs with characters who are positive role models.* Encourage your children to select programs with characters who are kind, caring, and cooperative. Such programs promote positive learning.
- *Do not rely on television as a baby-sitter.* Encourage your child to entertain himself in ways other than watching television. This will promote creativity.
- *Start limiting television viewing while your child is young.* If a child learns to limit television viewing at a young age, he is less likely to develop bad television-viewing habits.

- *Set specific rules about television viewing.* Determine ahead of time what programs your child will watch. Stick to the schedule!
- *Discuss violence.* If your child does view violence on television, discuss with him what he sees. Explain that the violence seen on television is "faked." Discuss the real-life consequences for such actions.
- *Get control of your own television viewing.* Set a good example. In most families, adults watch even more television than their children. Limit the amount of television you watch. Let your child see you reading and taking part in many activities other than watching television.
- *Know what your child is watching.* Whenever possible, preview the programs your child wants to watch. If you have a vcr, you could record the programs your child selects and then view them before he does.
- *Watch television with your child.* Be available to answer his questions and provide information. This will help promote learning.
- *Encourage other activities.* These may include reading, sports, and family activities.

Peer Influences

Your strong-willed child may select friends who are a bad influence. Children choose such friends for a number of different reasons. Some choose them for the attention they receive (from parents and other children), while others choose them for the excitement that accompanies breaking rules with the friends.

Fortunately, there are ways parents can reduce and correct such influences. The following guidelines can help you minimize the bad influence of peers:

- *Develop a close relationship with your child.* If your child has a close relationship with you, he is more likely to identify with you rather than with companions who are a bad influence.

- *Plan regular and frequent family activities.* Participate in regular, frequent family activities, such as picnics, hikes in the woods, and sports. If your child spends quality time with you, he is less likely to give in to peer pressure.
- *Encourage friendships with positive role models.* Encourage your child to develop and maintain friendships with children who have positive qualities. Invite these children over to play or to join the family for an outing.
- *Know your child's friends and their parents.* Spend time with your child's friends. Meet the parents of your child's friends.
- *Monitor your child's time with friends.* Do not let your child spend large amounts of time (for instance, sleepovers) with children you know are a bad influence. Don't allow your child to visit friends whose parents don't monitor their child's activities.
- *Do not criticize your child's friends.* Instead of criticizing friends, discuss specific behaviors of concern that occur when that child is a companion of your child.
- *Try to figure out the reason your child selects companions who are a bad influence, and then address it.* Your child may develop friendships with bad companions for many different reasons. Once you find the reasons, attempt to solve the problem.
- *Encourage a wide variety of friends.* Encourage your child to have many different friends. This will expose him to other children who have many different interests and ideas.
- *Encourage individuality and independence.* As your child grows older, stress the importance of being one's own person and doing what he feels is right for him.
- *Provide limits and enforce those limits.* If your child gets into trouble with a companion, apply appropriate consequences. Also, remember to praise him for the times he shows good judgment and stays out of trouble.

Tackling Your Family's Problems

As you can see from the examples discussed in this chapter, a number of factors can influence your parenting and your child's behavior. If you are not experiencing difficulties in these areas, count yourself as fortunate. Many parents do need to actively address one or more of these areas. If you are among them, first decide whether the problem area is so severe that you need professional help, and if you do, get it!

If not, focus first on the problem area you think can be solved most easily. Do not worry about any other problems—just direct all your energy and effort toward working out an acceptable solution for this one area. Once you have reached a solution, move to the next problem area and work on it. In this way, you can be focused rather than overwhelmed. Also, because you picked the easiest problem to solve first, you can enjoy your success and increase your motivation to address more difficult problems.

PART II

Addressing Strong-Willed Behavior: A Five-Week Program

At this point, you should better understand the various factors that contribute to your strong-willed child's behavior (Part I). This understanding can help you appreciate the next dimension of our strategy: learning parenting techniques to address problems associated with your child's strong-willed behavior. The chapters in Part II teach those techniques in the form of a five-week program.

Part II starts with a discussion about how you can decide whether your child's behavior needs to change (Chapter 4). We then present our five-week program. Each of the subsequent five chapters discusses a different skill, and you learn one skill per week. The skills build on each other, so it is important that you master each skill before moving to the next skill. Mastery of a skill involves more than simply understanding the skill and knowing what to do. It involves actually using the skill on a daily basis with your child. The skills you will be learning are attending (Chapter 5), rewarding (Chapter 6), ignoring (Chapter 7), giving your child effective directions (Chapter 8), and using time-out correctly (Chapter 9). Finally, in Chapter 10 we discuss how to integrate these skills to achieve maximum effectiveness in changing your child's behavior.

4

Does My Child's Behavior Really Need to Change?

> *"I have to tell Karen to pick up her toys at least ten times before she does it!"*

> *"Jimmy stamps his foot and yells 'no' when I tell him to take a bath."*

> *"Amanda is a terror in the grocery store—always demanding candy, running up and down the aisles, grabbing things, and throwing tantrums."*

> *"At supper Bob constantly picks at his sister. He mimics her, kicks her under the table, and interrupts her every time she tries to say something."*

> *"Tracy seems to know that, when I am on the phone, she can do whatever she wants to do, and I can't do anything about it."*

Do these statements sound like ones you make about your child? If so, using the five-week program presented in the following chapters will improve the problem behaviors of your strong-willed child and improve the relationship between the two of you. The skills you will learn are ones all parents should use. However, the program was originally developed and shown to be clinically effective with strong-willed children who have high rates of noncompliant and other disruptive behaviors. This chapter focuses on deciding whether you and your child need this program.

Problem Behaviors

One way to decide whether you need the five-week program is to evaluate whether your child often engages in types of behaviors that are problematic. Worksheet 4-1 lists more than a dozen problem behaviors—mainly the noncompliant and disruptive behaviors common among strong-willed children. While several of the behaviors listed on the worksheet, such as temper tantrums and stubbornness, are very common among strong-willed children, other behaviors such as lying and stealing occur less frequently. However, these more "severe" behavior problems can develop if the more common behavior problems associated with being strong-willed are not handled effectively and are allowed to escalate over time.

Using the box in front of each behavior, place a check next to each kind of behavior your child engages in at least occasionally. If your child shows many of these behaviors, the five-week program should be particularly beneficial.

Problem Situations

Another way to evaluate whether your strong-willed child's behavior warrants a systematic parenting intervention such as our five-week program is to consider how he behaves in situations that often present problems. To help you do this, Worksheet 4-2 lists a number of common situations in which parents frequently interact with two- to

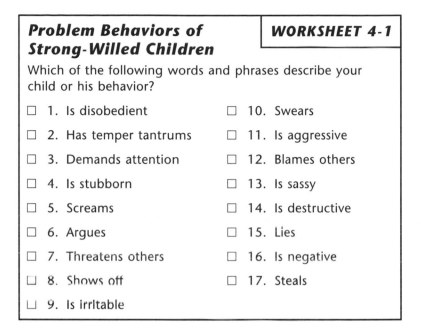

Problem Behaviors of Strong-Willed Children

WORKSHEET 4-1

Which of the following words and phrases describe your child or his behavior?

☐ 1. Is disobedient

☐ 2. Has temper tantrums

☐ 3. Demands attention

☐ 4. Is stubborn

☐ 5. Screams

☐ 6. Argues

☐ 7. Threatens others

☐ 8. Shows off

☐ 9. Is irritable

☐ 10. Swears

☐ 11. Is aggressive

☐ 12. Blames others

☐ 13. Is sassy

☐ 14. Is destructive

☐ 15. Lies

☐ 16. Is negative

☐ 17. Steals

six-year-old children. These situations focus on routine activities, such as going to bed at night, taking a bath, and grocery shopping.

In the blank next to each situation, indicate whether your child's behavior is a problem in that situation. Do you have difficulty with your child complying to your instructions in each situation? In the next blank, note how often your child is a problem in this situation. For example, think about putting your child to bed at night. Is it difficult getting your child to go to bed every night of the week or perhaps only one or two nights out of the week?

In the next two spaces, write down what typically happens in each problem situation. What do you do? What does your child do? Returning to the bedtime situation, do you tuck your child in bed and tell him "good night" but find he gets out of bed and comes into the den where you are watching television? If so, what do you then do? Do you put him back in bed or let him stay up? If you put him back to bed, does he get up again? If so, what do you

Situations in Which Strong-Willed Children Often Display Problems

WORKSHEET 4-2

Situation	Is There a Problem?	How Often?	What Do You Do?	What Does Your Child Do?
Going to Bed				
Getting Up in the Morning				
Mealtime				
Bathtime				
When You Are on Phone				
When You Have Visitors at Home				
When You Visit Others				
Riding in the Car				
Grocery Shopping				
Eating in Restaurants				

do then? For each problem situation list what your child does and what you do in response. Of particular importance is what happens at the end of the interaction. In the bedtime example, do you eventually give up and let your child stay up?

Complete Worksheet 4-2 for each situation for your strong-willed child. Many parents have found this to be an eye-opening experience. They discover that most of these routine situations involve problems with their child's behavior. That was true of the mother whose following words tell what happens when she is on the phone:

> "The minute I get on the phone with my mother or a friend, it's like Steve's antenna goes up, and he realizes he can get away with anything. He torments his sister, jumps on the sofa, crawls up on the kitchen counter to grab candy, and starts throwing things out of the refrigerator. It's incredible, and I'm trapped in a conversation and can only helplessly watch him and become more and more frustrated. I now dread the phone ringing!"

Some parents experience problems with their child in only one or two of the situations presented in Worksheet 4-2. If you are one of these parents, spending five weeks in the parenting program is one way—and a very good way—to solve these problems and improve your overall relationship with your child. However, most parents we have encountered experience problems with their child in many of the situations. This behavior pattern suggests problems in the general interactions between parent and child. Under these circumstances, it is very important to use the five-week program to change these general interactions, rather than trying to solve each problem situation individually. Improvement in the general interactions solves many of the individual problems with a strong-willed child. This happens because the child becomes more cooperative overall and, thus, more willing to do what the parent requests. At the same time, the parent gains a general set of skills to use with different problem situations that may arise. In other words, the five-week program will help you acquire skills to be a problem solver in many difficult situations with your strong-willed child.

Degree of Compliance

Another way to determine the magnitude of your child's problem behaviors is to stage an interaction with him. This will give you some firsthand information about the difficulties between you and your child. All you need for this interaction is a few toys and some time alone with your child. You give your child a series of directions and see if he complies with your requests. Strong-willed children typically are not very compliant!

Mark Roberts, a psychologist at Idaho State University, has developed a standard set of directions, called the Compliance Test, which parents can use to examine how compliant their child is. These thirty directions are presented in Table 4-1. To administer this test, you tell your child that you want him to do some things for you. You lay out the toys described in the directions in Table 4-1, then issue the directions exactly as they are presented. Do not say or do anything else. Record whether or not your child complies within five seconds, then issue the next direction. Continue until you have issued all thirty directions. You may substitute other toys for those specified.

You probably will observe several things as you issue the directions. First, your child may comply less often as you issue more directions. This is common, so don't be surprised. Second, very few children comply with all of the directions. Therefore, you should not expect perfect compliance; it is unrealistic.

How do you know if your child has a problem with compliance? If he complies less than 60 percent of the time (eighteen of the thirty directions), you will have reason to

Compliance Test Directions	TABLE 4-1

Toys Needed: cat, bear, dog, frog, box, 3 cars, dump truck, house, rabbit, person, 2 blocks. (Note: Substitutions with other toys are acceptable.

1. Put this cat in the box.
2. Put this bear in the box.
3. Put this frog in the box.
4. Put this dog in the box.
5. Put this rabbit in the box.
6. Put this block in the truck.
7. Put this car in the truck.
8. Put this person in the truck.
9. Put this block in the truck.
10. Put this animal in the truck.
11. Put this car in the house.
12. Put this person in the house.
13. Put this block in the house.
14. Put this animal in the house.
15. Put this car in the house.
16. Put this car in the box.
17. Put this person in the box.
18. Put this block in the box.
19. Put this animal in the box.
20. Put this person in the box.
21. Put this cat in the box.
22. Put this bear in the box.
23. Put this frog in the box.
24. Put this dog in the box.
25. Put this rabbit in the box.
26. Put this car in the truck.
27. Put this car in the truck.
28. Put this car in the truck.
29. Put this block in the truck.
30. Put this block in the truck.

Source: Mark W. Roberts, Professor of Psychology, Idaho State University. Reprinted with permission.

question how compliant he is. However, you should consider other factors as well. For example, does he talk back to you ("You can't make me do it"), become aggressive, or sulk? All of these behaviors, as well as his actual compliance, should provide you with valuable information about your child's behavior and the extent to which he is strong-willed. Not surprisingly, parents whose children score low on the compliance test have reports such as these about their child's routine behavior:

> "It's so frustrating! I can't get Mark to bed at night, and then I can't get him up in the morning. I tell him to get up, I shake him, I keep going back into his room, but he just will not get up. I finally sit him up in bed and dress him while he screams and pouts. By then we are both foul and it is so late that breakfast is horrible and rushed. Who would have ever thought that both of us would start out almost every day this way!"

> "Tracy is amazing—she never wants to take a bath, but once she gets in the tub, I can't get her out! As soon as I say that it's bathtime, she screams and runs. I have to literally fight with her to undress her and then almost drag her to the tub. Once she is in the water, she's fine until it's time to get out. The fight then starts all over again! I have to drag her out kicking and screaming and try to dry off and dress an irritable child who cries and acts like she's dying!"

Let's look for a moment at why we pay special attention to child compliance and noncompliance. Several clinical researchers have suggested that noncompliance is the cornerstone of behavior problems for young children. What does this mean? First, noncompliance is the most frequently occurring behavior problem among young children. Second, and perhaps even more important, noncompliance is the problem behavior that sets the stage for other problem behaviors. That is, if child noncompliance is not a problem early on, the child also is unlikely to engage in behaviors that may be problems in the pre-school years or even later on. These other problem behaviors build upon the original behavior of noncompliance. Thus, it is important to determine if noncompliance is a primary problem behavior of your child—which is likely among strong-willed children.

Let's return to the situations in Worksheet 4-2. Is your child noncompliant in most of these situations? For example, does he fail to comply when you instruct him to go to bed, come to the dinner table, or get out of the bathtub? Each of these situations represents a time when you are trying to have your child comply with directions. Furthermore, in both the daily situations (Worksheet 4-2) and the Compliance Test (Table 4-1), your child may demonstrate some of the problem behaviors listed in Worksheet 4-1. For example, he may argue, scream, and become aggressive. As you probably are beginning to see, all of the ways we have presented to examine your child's behavior fit together to form a picture of a strong-willed child!

Your Frustration Level

There is one final test for you to consider when trying to decide if you should undertake the five-week program. This one is very easy and requires only a few minutes of careful thought. Answer this one question: Am I often frustrated by my child's behavior and by my failure to help my child behave better? If the answer is yes, you are a parent who wants something better for your child and for yourself. The five-week parenting program is for you!

Introduction to the Five-Week Program

The Five-Week Program for Addressing Strong-Willed Behavior consists of five parenting skills to be learned one skill at a time. The skills build on one another, so it is important to master the first skill before moving to the second skill. Mastering a skill involves more than simply understanding the skill and knowing what to do; you must actually use the skill on a daily basis with your child. That is why you learn only one skill per week. Believe it or not, it takes at least a week to master a new parenting skill and make it part of your daily repertoire!

Thus, in the five-week program you will be exposed to a skill and then practice that skill daily over the course of a week. Once you have mastered the skill, which should require a week but could well take longer, you move on to the next skill. However, you do *not* move on until you have mastered the skill. This is the strength of the Five-Week Program for Addressing Strong-Willed Behavior—it involves actual behavior change on the part of you and your child.

With each skill you will be learning, it is far more effective if *both* mother and father in two-parent homes undertake the five-week program. If both of you go through the program together, you can expect greater improvement in your child's behavior as well as improved relationships among all family members. Furthermore, if both of you participate, you can practice skills with each other before you try them with your child. One parent can play the role of the child, and the other parent can play the role of the parent. One parent practices the skills, and then the roles are reversed. This might be uncomfortable at first, but it can greatly enhance your opportunity to learn the skill and to use it consistently and effectively with your child.

The Smith and Jones Families

To help you see the types of problems experienced by other families with a strong-willed child and how the five-week program can help, let's look at two hypothetical families. We'll call them the Smiths and the Joneses. We will follow both families throughout the five-week program.

The Smith Family

John and Barbara Smith grew up together in a small town in the Midwest. They began dating in high school, then while Barbara attended the local community college, John attended a state university about three hours away. During the first two years of college, Barbara and John continued to date; after their second year of college, they decided to marry. Barbara assumed a position as a secretary while John continued his education at the state university. When John completed his degree in business two years later, the Smiths moved to a city in a neighboring state so John could take a job in sales with a young but growing company.

Almost immediately after the move, to the delight of both Barbara and John, Barbara became pregnant. Nine months later Susan was born. During the next two years, Barbara devoted herself to being a homemaker and caring for Susan. John worked long hours, but everyone who knew him could tell that his family was an important priority.

Shortly after Susan's second birthday, again to the delight of both of the Smiths, Barbara became pregnant again. Nine months later Tim was born. Almost immediately Barbara and John noted that Tim was a very different baby than Susan had been. Whereas Susan would lie in her bed cooing or play contentedly on the floor, Tim often was cranky, slept poorly at night, and was difficult to feed, as he would take small amounts of milk and then cry and spit it up. When Susan was an infant, Barbara would cheerfully greet John at the door when he returned home from work. At the same stage of Tim's life, she often was irritated, tired, and frustrated when John arrived home. John's role in the evening changed from one of relaxing, casually playing with his daughter, recounting his day in detail, and listening to Susan to one of assuming many of the responsibilities with Tim in the evening. Throughout the night John and Barbara would alternate who would respond to Tim's crying, which occurred every two to three hours.

Over the next two years, Tim's behavior changed, but unfortunately it did not improve. Instead of crying to be picked up, Tim was crawling and walking around the house destroying magazines, framed pictures, and his sister's dolls. Barbara found herself becoming the "No" Mommy. In her own words, "It seemed like every time I had something to say to Tim, it began with 'No, don't do that Tim.'" Barbara found herself spanking Tim more and more, creating excuses to leave the house as soon as John came home, and having recurring thoughts like "I love Tim, but I sure do not like him!" These thoughts usually were followed by feelings of guilt, especially when Tim was asleep at night.

Shortly after Tim turned two and a half, Barbara became pregnant again. In contrast to their feelings about the first two pregnancies, neither John nor Barbara was excited. In fact, both of them wondered how they would be able to handle another child when Tim's strong-willed behavior took so much effort and time. Furthermore, although they both thought of Susan as their "perfect child," they were concerned that with another child she would receive even less attention than she had since Tim's birth.

Beyond their concerns with their two children, Barbara and John were not doing so well themselves. Barbara was frequently moody and depressed, whereas John worked longer hours and was more irritable during the time that he did spend at home. He often snapped at Barbara, and he spent less and less time with both of the children. He fussed about how disorganized the house was, saying, "I can't deal with all my work stress and the mess at home."

During the early stages of her third pregnancy, Barbara was frequently sick and had little energy. During this time, Tim's behavior problems appeared to accelerate. It seemed that he was constantly picking at his sister, screaming, "You can't make me do it!" at his mother, refusing to comply with even the simplest instruction from either parent, and requiring hours to go to sleep at night. His behavior outside the home with his parents was no better. In the grocery store, Tim would break away from his mother and run through the aisles. When Barbara would catch up with him, he would immediately start screaming and fall down on the floor, having a full blown tantrum. Because of her pregnancy and Tim's size, Barbara simply could not handle him in public places. As a result, all trips outside the home with Tim were limited to times when his father could be present. In fact, all trips outside the home were limited to those that were absolutely necessary!

During this time Barbara and John finally brought themselves to the realization that Tim's strong-willed behavior was a problem that they must address. Furthermore, Barbara and John realized that their home environment was not the positive one it used to be. Playing with the children, having family talks around the kitchen table, watching television together, and enjoying picnics as a family in the park just were not occurring anymore. The fun times were gone, and family life had become a chore. As a result, John and Barbara decided to make a concerted effort together to improve Tim's behavior and make their home a more positive place for everyone. Just making that decision raised their spirits and their enthusiasm for their family.

The Jones Family

Ed and Patricia Jones met during their third year of college, when they were in the same journalism class at a private university on the East Coast. Although they had very different interests, each was attracted to the other. Ed enjoyed sports, parties, and large groups of friends. In contrast, Patricia enjoyed watching movies at home and romantic dinners. Nevertheless, Ed and Patricia were head over heels in love, and as soon as they completed college, they married.

Ed and Patricia moved to a large city on the West Coast, where Ed took a position with a large firm and Patricia became a freelance writer. She became successful almost immediately based on several articles published in popular magazines. In fact, her success appeared to put a distance between Ed and her, as he received little recognition and no promotions in his firm.

When Patricia became pregnant at twenty-nine years of age, it appeared to improve her relationship with Ed. For the first time in several years, they had a common goal: raising a child. When Lisa was born, Patricia and Ed assumed the role of doting parents. Perhaps surprisingly, Lisa responded positively to her parents' excessive attention and was viewed by everyone as a "sweet" child.

Patricia's life revolved around Lisa and her continuing success as a freelance writer. Feeling excluded from the relationship between Lisa and her mother, as well as unable to share Patricia's career success, Ed distanced himself from the family. He soon returned to activities he had enjoyed before marriage, spending his extra time at sporting events and local bars.

Patricia and Ed began to quarrel more frequently about his behavior. At first these quarrels occurred when Lisa was asleep; however, they soon began to spill over into the rest of the day and would occur in front of her. Finally, Ed and Patricia agreed to separate. Eventually, they divorced. Lisa was now four and a half years old.

The divorce was not easy for any of the Joneses. Ed appeared to be even less interested in Lisa than he had been, and Patricia became more involved in her work and a new romantic relationship. However, no one changed more than Lisa; she was no longer viewed as a "sweet" child but rather as a "strong-willed" child. Once Lisa decided to do something, there was nothing that Patricia could do to change her mind. Furthermore, she typically refused to do even the simplest activities that enable a single parent and child to get through a typical day. Lisa refused to put on her coat in the morning when leaving for preschool, refused to get out of the car when they arrived at the preschool, refused to take a bath, and disrupted her mother constantly with questions and demands whenever Patricia was on the telephone. Patricia found herself coaxing, pleading, demanding, threatening, and, at times, screaming at Lisa—none of which worked.

At first Patricia thought Lisa's behavior would settle down with time. However, after six months, Patricia realized her behavior was becoming worse, not better. Patricia knew that she needed to do more than wait for Lisa to "grow out of her bad behavior."

5

Week 1: Attending

The first skill in the five-week parenting program is attending—describing your child's appropriate behavior and, at times, imitating what your child is doing. In many ways, it is one of the most important skills because it lays the groundwork for a more positive relationship between you and your child. Building on this relationship, you can learn the remaining skills more effectively, and your child's behavior can improve more significantly. Attending is really very simple. It allows you to tune in to your child's behavior and lets your child know that you are very interested in the positive things he does. If you think about your strong-willed child's behavior, many of your thoughts may focus on the negative aspects. Attending will give you a chance to reverse this situation by noticing some of his positive behaviors.

To see how important this is, think about bosses for whom you have worked. How did they relate to you and other employees? Try to think of the top three characteristics of the supervisor for whom you *most* enjoyed working and the top three characteristics of the supervisor for whom you *least* enjoyed working. When people list such characteristics, they often come up with surprisingly similar answers. Characteristics of the "worst" supervisors include being overly negative, taking their employees for granted, and not being understanding. The "best" supervisors are often described as being appreciative of employees' work, being understanding and warm, and providing employees with a lot of positive feedback. Research shows that employees whose supervisors provide positive feedback are not only happier in their jobs but also more productive. Your role in the parent-child relationship is much like that of a supervisor.

When you think about your relationship with your child, how would you describe your characteristics as a "supervisor"? Many parents of strong-willed children fall into a cycle in which they become overly negative and provide less than optimal levels of warmth and positive feedback. Strong-willed children may perceive, often accurately, that their parents always notice their inappropriate behavior but rarely notice or acknowledge their appropriate behavior. So they continue to behave inappropriately, and their parents become more and more negative. In contrast, parents who learn and use the attending skill are perceived as warmer and more aware of a child's appropriate behavior. Through the use of attending skills, parents improve the way they relate to their children, which can result in their children becoming not only more contented but also more willing to cooperate.

The Role of Attending

When parents use the attending skill, it communicates that they do notice and are interested in their child's appropriate behavior. If a positive home environment exists (see Chapter 11), a child will value his parents' attention. Under these conditions, attending to appropriate behavior will increase the likelihood that he will behave appropriately more of the time.

Here are some examples of how a parent attends to a child's behavior:

- "My, you're stacking the blocks high!"
- "You're putting the yellow block on top of the blue block!"
- "Now you're driving the truck!"
- "You're turning the truck around in a circle!"
- "You're coloring the picture red!"
- "You're coloring the sky blue!"
- "You're lining up all the toys!"
- "You're putting the ball next to the bucket!"
- "You're blowing up the balloon!"
- "The balloon is getting so big!"
- "Whoops, the balloon broke!"

Notice that the parent gives no directions and asks no questions. The parent simply describes exactly what the child is doing. Also notice that there is an exclamation point after each statement. This means that the attends are stated with positive emotion and enthusiasm.

Beyond describing, a parent also may be imitating what her child is doing. For example, if he is stacking blocks, the parent may also stack blocks. Imitation not only communicates approval of the child's behavior but also teaches young children how to play with others.

Attending sounds simple. However, most parents of strong-willed children do not spend much time just paying attention to their child's appropriate behavior. Rather, their interactions primarily involve directions and questions. Such an interaction style indicates that parents of a strong-willed child typically are interested in having their child respond to them by behaving as directed or answering questions. Many parents interact with their strong-willed child almost exclusively by using directions and questions. In addition, these parents often fail to follow up on the directions by making sure their child complies or to follow up on the questions by waiting for an answer. As a result, a strong-willed child tends to tune his parents out and over time complies to directions and responds to questions less and less often. Unfortunately, the more a child tunes out his parents, the more directions and questions parents feel they need to issue in order to try to gain compliance just once in a while. As you can see, a vicious circle begins: the less a child responds, the more directions and questions a parent issues; the more directions and questions a parent issues, the less the child responds!

To improve interactions with your strong-willed child, you must change this negative cycle of issuing many directions and questions and rarely receiving compliance or answers. Using attends is the first step. This chapter will allow you to learn the skill and, later in the week, begin applying it to your daily interactions with your child.

The Smith and Jones Families

Let's first observe how the Smith and Jones families learned to incorporate attending into their daily lives.

The Smith Family

John and Barbara Smith were concerned about Tim's strong-willed behavior. They had decided to try making changes in his behavior and in their family life. They realized that in about four months, when their third child was due, it would be difficult to find the time and energy to focus primarily on Tim's behavior. Now was the time for change!

One of these changes was to become more positive with Tim, and both of the Smiths realized that attending was an excellent way to do this. Barbara and John read about attending skills. Initially, John felt that describing Tim's behavior over and over sounded rather silly. However, he said, "I'll try anything," and agreed to practice the attending skills with Barbara so they could both learn how to use attending.

The attending skills were harder for Barbara and John to learn than they first expected. Both parents caught themselves asking questions ("What are you doing?") and telling Tim what to do, rather than simply describing his activity during playtimes. At first Barbara, who was with Tim more than John, was more committed to her practice sessions with their son. However, John was more than willing to observe Barbara practicing with Tim. At these times he noticed how many questions and instructions she used in the interaction. This made him think about his own behavior with Tim. He began to realize that, at the dinner table, during bathtime, and when playing ball outside, almost everything he said to his son was a question or a direction to do something.

As John observed more of the play sessions between Barbara and Tim, he also realized that, as Barbara's behavior became more positive and attentive and less demanding and questioning, Tim appeared to enjoy his mother's company more and played in a less rambunctious and more cooperative manner. Watching Barbara and Tim led John to conclude, "Maybe there *is* something to this attending business." At the same time, Barbara was having a similar reaction to her own experiences in using the attending skills with Tim and her observations of John and Tim in their increasingly frequent play sessions.

Barbara and John began discussing ways to use attending at times other than during designated playtimes with Tim and to use the skills with his older sister, Susan. Barbara found that, if she brought Tim's toys into the kitchen, he would play on the floor with them while she described his activities and cooked dinner. Susan also was responsive to Barbara's attending. In fact, she would grin at her mother and say, "I like being with you, Mommy." John began using attending skills when he and Tim went grocery shopping. Instead of listening to the radio, John turned it off and described the scenery along the roadside to Tim; he also described his son's behavior. Tim's behavior changed almost immediately from constant squirming and trying to get out of his seat belt to listening and talking with his father.

John and Barbara began to realize that using attending was exactly the opposite of what they had been doing. In the past, when Tim was acting up, they would usually attend to him, most of the time in a negative way. Whenever he was behaving appropriately, they had been adhering to the philosophy of "let sleeping dogs (children) lie." John said, "Tim was good so seldom that, whenever he was good, we weren't going to say anything because he might quit."

Barbara and John realized that the attending skill was designed to tune them in to Tim's good behavior. The more they did this, the more they realized that Tim was not always bad, and they actually enjoyed being with him, at least some of the time. There were still many difficult times, and Tim continued to be strong-willed when it came to complying with his parents' instructions. However, at least they had made a start. Something positive was happening in the Smith family.

The Jones Family

Patricia Jones was having increasing problems with Lisa's strong-willed behavior after she and Ed divorced. Attending was particularly difficult for Patricia, largely because, as a single mom, she could not find time periods to practice the attending skills with Lisa. She had not realized the amount of time and effort required to become more child-focused. After all, her life was busy, and Ed had transferred to the East Coast for a long-awaited promotion. Although they never discussed it, both of the Joneses knew that raising Lisa was Patricia's sole responsibility. Patricia was glad to avoid the hassles over child rearing that many of her divorced friends and their ex-spouses were experiencing; however, she was apprehensive about the challenges of dealing alone with a strong-willed child.

Nevertheless, Patricia knew that she had to practice the attending skills in order to master them and for Lisa's behavior to change. She soon realized that extra time to practice the skill was not necessary. Instead, she began having practice sessions at times when she was already with Lisa. She practiced attending with her daughter in the car while going to and from Lisa's day-care center, and she practiced the skills at night when she and Lisa ate dinner together. At first, Lisa was not too enthused about this because it involved turning off the TV so that she and her mother could focus on each other. However, as her mother's attention increased, Lisa's insistence on watching TV diminished and finally dropped out altogether.

For Patricia, the importance of the attending skill took on added significance when she began receiving national attention for some of her work. A close friend and confidant, who was aware of Patricia's use of attending, stated, "You seem to like people to attend to you as much as Lisa likes you to attend to her." With that comment, Patricia had an "aha" experience; she suddenly realized what positive attention can mean to anyone, including Lisa.

Lisa's behavior began to become less difficult. Lisa and Patricia enjoyed more positive times together, such as lying on the bed and giggling and laughing together. Getting in the car to go to preschool became less of a hassle as Patricia began not only attending to Lisa getting ready but also planning ways to avoid problems. She found that she could avoid confrontations by letting Lisa know what to expect (saying, for example, "In about five minutes, we will leave for school, and you will need to put on your coat"). Patricia also found that she was enjoying her time with Lisa more and more. Lisa still demanded attention and wanted to do things her own way, but the good times seemed to be occurring more and more often.

Learning to Attend

The most effective way to learn attending skills is to set aside specific practice sessions. During these practice sessions, the parent describes aloud what the child is doing.

When a parent is attending well during a practice session, anyone overhearing should be able to tell exactly what the child is doing. Attending is very similar to a sportscaster giving a play-by-play commentary of a sporting event. During initial practice sessions, many parents felt almost silly using the attending skill because it makes them sound childlike. In fact, this is exactly how we want you to sound!

To get started with your practice sessions, set aside at least two ten-minute periods per day. These are times

Two Styles of Interacting

Here are two transcripts of interactions between a parent and a child. In the first interaction the parent mainly gives directions and asks questions. In the second interaction the parent uses only attends. Parental directions, questions, and attends are marked with a *(d)* for a direction, a *(q)* for a question, or an *(a)* for an attend.

Interaction Dominated by Directions and Questions

Parent: Let's play now. (d)
Child: OK.
Parent: What do you want to play? (q)
Child: I don't know.
Parent: Well, we don't have long. Decide now. (d)
Child: Let's play blocks.
Parent: That will be fun.
Child: I know.
Parent: Move them over here so we can play. (d)
Child: OK.
Parent: Why don't you make a castle. (d)
Child: OK.
Parent: You are really stacking the blocks high. (a)
Child: I know.
Parent: So, do you think you can make a castle like in the picture? (q)
Child: I don't know.
Parent: Well, try to make one. (d)
Child: I will.
Parent: Then you should put the big blocks on the bottom. (d)

Interaction Dominated by Attends

Parent: You're ready to play now! (a)

Child: I sure am.

Parent: Yesterday you built a big fort.

Child: Yes! Today I'm going to build a castle.

Parent: That will be great!

Child: Yeah.

Parent: Now you're putting the brown blocks in a big circle! (a)

Child: They will be my moat.

Parent: Boy, you sure can build high walls! (a)

Child: Now I'm going to build a tower.

Parent: Wow, you're making it so tall. (a)

Child: I hope it doesn't fall down.

Parent: You're putting up some neat buildings inside the castle. (a)

Child: Yeah, they're for the soldiers to sleep in.

Parent: And now you put in a gate! (a)

Child: The king and all his men need a gate to get in.

The differences may appear subtle, but this parent is communicating two very different messages to her child. In the first dialogue the parent is communicating that she is in charge and that her agenda, not the child's, is most important. In the second dialogue the parent is communicating that she is interested in her child and his activities.

when you and your child can sit down in a play situation without being interrupted. Finding such practice times is difficult for today's busy families. However, it is *absolutely necessary* for you to do if you are going to effectively learn the attending skill, as it will be for learning the other skills. To improve your strong-willed child's behavior, you have to make both the quantity and quality of time you spend with your child a high priority so you can learn the skills effectively. We call this becoming "child-focused." Once you complete the program, you will be able to decrease some of your focus on your child; however, you may not *want* to decrease this focus. You may find being with your child is much more pleasant and rewarding than it ever was!

Within each ten-minute practice session, sit down on the floor with your child and have a number of toys available for play. Tell your child that you want to play whatever he wants to play (within reason). During the playtime, your job is to describe your child's appropriate behavior with attending statements. If he displays minor inappropriate behavior during the practice session, try to ignore such behavior. Besides attending to appropriate behavior, you also may imitate your child's play behavior, but in doing so, you should not guide or structure his activities. Like describing, imitation says, "I am interested in you and what you are doing." Of equal importance, you should *not* use directions and questions during the practice sessions. This is your child's time to direct the activity.

If you are like many parents of strong-willed children, you may be so accustomed to giving directions and asking questions that you are not even aware of how much you are interacting with your child in this way. As a result, it can be very helpful to tape-record your practice time with your child and listen to it later. Or you can have your spouse or someone else note the number of attends, directions, and questions you give in the practice session. In either case, you may be surprised at how many directions and questions you use.

When parents begin trying to use fewer directions and questions during these play interactions with their child, they often have a hard time thinking of how to turn what they instinctively want to say into attends. In the practice situation, you need to carefully think about each statement you are about to make. Thus, if you think about saying, "Are you stacking the blocks?" you can change the question into an attend statement by simply saying, "Now you're stacking the blocks!" Such a statement demands nothing of your child but lets him know that you are interested in his activities.

Continue the two ten-minute practice sessions with your child for seven days. (Sorry, but there are no weekends or holidays for parents!) After each practice session,

Guidelines for Practice Sessions: Attending	**TABLE 5-1**

Do Not	*Do*
Issue any instructions	Attend to (describe) your child's appropriate behavior
Ask any questions	Imitate your child's play behavior
	Tape-record the session or have someone observe the session
	Evaluate your performance
	Reward yourself for your efforts and performance

listen to the tape recording of the session or receive feedback from the person who observed the session. Just as you do with your child, focus on the positive parts of your performance. Do not be overly critical; you are learning a new approach to parenting, and it will take time. Reward yourself for taking the time, putting forth the effort, and improving your performance on the way to becoming a better parent. Pat yourself on the back, compliment yourself, take a leisurely stroll, watch your favorite television comedy show—do something pleasant and reinforcing for yourself. Parenting is hard work, and your efforts should be rewarded!

The guidelines for the attending practice sessions are summarized in Table 5-1.

After day 3, you will need to take on a second assignment. Find two "natural times" during the day to use attends with your child for at least five minutes. This might be while you are riding in the car with your child, sitting with him while he takes a bath, or grocery shopping together. All of these, as well as many other daily interactions with your child, are excellent times to begin incorporating the attending skill into your daily routine. It is only when the skill becomes a natural part of your daily interactions with your strong-willed child that his behavior and your relationship with him will begin to improve.

Finally, after day 4 and continuing for the rest of the week, pick a one-hour period when you and your child are both at home together. This may be late in the afternoon or during the evening after dinner. Your job is to give your child at least twenty attends during this hour. Some parents have bought a golf wristcounter in order to keep up with how many attends they give and to remind themselves that they are supposed to be attending during these practice times. These parents have reported that wearing the counter really helped them remember to provide frequent attends. If you prefer, substitute another reminder, such as a rubber band on the wrist.

Worksheet 5-1 outlines the daily requirements for you this week in terms of learning and using the attending skill. Use the spaces provided in the worksheet to check off when you have completed each day's assignment.

Daily Assignments for Week 1: Attending	**WORKSHEET 5-1**						
				Days			
Tasks	1	2	3	4	5	6	7
1. Two 10-minute practice times	☐	☐	☐	☐	☐	☐	☐
2. Two 5-minute natural times				☐	☐	☐	☐
3. One-hour period: 20 attends					☐	☐	☐

Practicing Your New Skill

You may be thinking, "Should I never issue another direction to my child or ask him another question?" By no means is this the case. Your child has to do many things every day of the week you are learning the attending skill. At those times, you should continue to issue directions to your child. Furthermore, there are many times you will want to ask your child a question. However, when you do this, be sure to listen to his answer. Why ask a question if you are not willing to wait for an answer? Whenever you want to ask a question or give a direction, consider whether your interactions with your strong-willed child involve too many directions and questions. Many times an attend is just as appropriate as a direction or question and far more effective in improving your relationship with your child.

If this seems difficult, don't despair. The Five-Week Program for Addressing Strong-Willed Behavior does involve substantial effort on your part. As one of our grandfathers used to say, "There is no substitute for hard work!" Clearly, parenting is hard work, and changing the way you parent is even harder. Try to reward yourself every several days for accomplishing the assignments. Treat yourself to a video, a special lunch, or something else you enjoy. When you successfully complete the first week of the program, do something *really* special for yourself. You deserve it!

It is also important to learn the parenting skill in a play situation with your child. The only way to have the skill become part of your daily routine is to learn it in a structured situation—the play situation—and after that to begin using the skill throughout the day. We are not just trying to teach you how to play with your child. Play is important, but attending is a skill to use throughout the day to let your child know you are interested in and acknowledge his appropriate behavior.

Please focus only on attending for the next seven days. Resist the temptation to read the next chapters! This program is most effective when you learn and practice only one skill at a time. Each subsequent skill builds on the previous skills. Parents who try to rush through the program and try to learn all the skills at once are often ineffective in changing the negative aspects of their child's strong-willed behavior. Your child's strong-willed behavior did not develop quickly, and it is not going to be changed quickly. Patience is very important!

6

Week 2: Rewards

When you practice and use the attending skill, you are simply describing or imitating what your child does while he is playing or engaged in some other activity. The next skill you will learn—rewards—is designed to make sure your child knows you approve of what he is doing. Rewards do not replace attends but rather build upon them. In other words, you should still describe your child's positive behavior but on some occasions move beyond this by also praising or rewarding it.

In this chapter we will describe the kinds of rewards that are most important and explain how you can learn to use rewards effectively. In general, rewards may be social rewards or nonsocial rewards (see Table 6-1). Social rewards can be either verbal, physical, or activities.

Verbal Rewards

Of all the rewards for young children, the most important are the verbal rewards. These rewards consist of praising a child's behavior and labeling exactly what your child did that you liked. For example, you might say, "Thank you for picking up your toys!" Think about that statement. Not only is the child being praised, but he also is being told

Types of Rewards	TABLE 6-1

Social Rewards

- Verbal: Praising your child's desirable behavior
- Physical: Physical contact (e.g., pat on back) following your child's desirable behavior
- Activities: Doing activities selected by your child following his desirable behavior

Nonsocial Rewards

- Toys or treats following your child's desirable behavior

the exact activity he did (picking up the toys) for which he is being praised. Here are some other verbal rewards:

- "I like it when you come to dinner when I call!"
- "I'm proud of you for playing so quietly!"
- "Thank you for picking up your blocks!"
- "I really like it when you obey me!"
- "Wow, you really did a great job of cleaning up your room!"
- "Thanks for helping me cook supper!"
- "I am really proud of you for doing such good school-work!"
- "You are a super kid for playing so nicely with your sister!"
- "Bob, I really appreciate that you came the first time I called you!"
- "I really noticed how hard you tried to stay by my side on our shopping trip!"
- "You popped right out of bed this morning when I called you! Thanks!"

In all of these cases, you are praising your child and labeling the desired behavior that occurred.

For preschool children, this is extremely important. Parents need to be positive with children, but we also need to let them know exactly which behaviors we are praising. The more information and feedback we can provide to our children when we talk to them, the more they are going to learn appropriate behavior.

On some occasions you may not have the time or feel the need to label your child's exact behavior. In these cases, you can use brief verbal rewards. Examples of these rewards include "good job," "great," and "thanks." Again, each of these statements lets your child know that you approve of and are proud of his behavior. However, these general statements tend to be less effective.

For many of us, verbal rewards do not come naturally. Therefore, you might want to write on a notecard some examples that might apply to your child. Keep the card with you and look at your list occasionally. This will help you remember ways to praise your child when he is behaving appropriately.

To give verbal rewards effectively, you have to consider not only *what* to say but also *how* to say it. Deliver praise in a pleased, enthusiastic tone of voice. Some of us are not very expressive. If you happen to be this way, work on becoming more expressive when you are praising your child. A positive statement such as "I really like it when you pick up your toys" is not very reinforcing if delivered in a flat, dull, monotone voice. Think about how you express yourself when you are really excited about something. That is how you should praise your child.

Physical Rewards

The second type of social reward is a physical reward such as a pat on the back, an arm on your child's shoulder, or a wink at your child. These are physical ways of letting your child know that you like the behavior he is displaying. Hugs and kisses also can be used as physical rewards; however, it is better to use these expressions of love frequently with our children than to reserve them for rewards.

Think about how much positive physical contact you

actually have with your strong-willed child. We have worked with many parents who do not like their child's behavior and therefore do not engage in much physical contact. If you are one of these parents, begin working on this by gently touching your child on the shoulder sometimes or patting him on the back. A simple wink or a playful tap can be very meaningful to a child. A realistic goal is to try to have twenty more touches per day with your child than you now have. You will be surprised how effective this can be.

Activity Rewards

The third type of social reward is an activity—doing things with your child that he really likes to do. When children have behavior problems, their parents tend to interact with their child only when they have to. As you might guess, these times usually involve required tasks like bathing, meals, and bedtime. Unfortunately, this eliminates any chance for pleasant interactions around some activity your child enjoys. Using an activity he enjoys as a reward can be very reinforcing for your child. It also gives you a chance to discover positive things about your child. Activity rewards might include playing a game, reading a story, or going on a walk. These activities can occur after your child has done something positive, such as picking up his toys or showing perseverance with a difficult task. But don't use these types of activities just as rewards. Make time for fun activities with your child. You will both enjoy yourselves and improve your relationship.

Activity rewards are a basic way of becoming more child-focused. This is important for you as a parent. The more you can focus on your child and become "childlike" in your own behaviors, the more you will enjoy your child, improve your relationship, and even find your strong-willed child is more eager to cooperate with you. Becoming "childlike" means doing things with your child that he enjoys doing—activities such as stacking blocks, going on a walk, throwing a football, playing with dolls, or playing Nintendo. With all of these activities, you have to let go and get down on your child's level.

How do you decide what is a rewarding activity for your child? One way is to recall the things your child has asked you to do with him. Another is to simply ask him what he enjoys doing. You also might generate a list of activity rewards and let him know that these are things the two of you can do together whenever he completes certain tasks.

Nonsocial Rewards

Along with the three types of social rewards are nonsocial rewards—desirable objects such as toys or special treats. These types of rewards are sometimes useful when you start teaching a new behavior. However, nonsocial rewards should always be combined with praise. What is most important to your young child is *your* attention. In other words, simply giving a child a toy for good behavior will not be very effective in changing his behavior. Rather, your attention in the form of social rewards is most important and should be naturally linked to using nonsocial rewards.

The Smith and Jones Families

Let's rejoin the Smith and Jones families. In learning the skill of rewarding, they faced several challenges. However, they also enjoyed some successes.

The Smith Family

When we last visited Barbara and John Smith, they were beginning to experience more positive times with Tim and had realized the importance of describing Tim's good behavior. In contrast to the notion of attending, which was new to the Smiths, the notion of rewards certainly was not novel. Both John and Barbara had read about the importance of rewards for positive behavior in various magazine articles about children. However, they had primarily thought of rewards as candy and toys, which they viewed as bribes for good behavior. The idea that attention served as a reward for children and adults was less familiar to them, and the idea that rewards were not bribery also was novel. In particular, Barbara and John had never understood that the way to teach children to behave appropriately is to initially use rewards frequently for small changes in behavior, gradually require more behavior change, and, once the behavior is learned, decrease the rewards as the behavior becomes internally controlled.

Barbara and John found it easy to incorporate rewards into their daily practice sessions with Tim. However, incorporating rewards into their daily routines was more difficult. In particular, both of the Smiths continued to think about disciplining negative behavior rather than focusing on Tim's less frequent positive behaviors. The two of them had to work together to develop a systematic plan before they could gradually change their focus from the negative to the positive aspects of Tim's behavior.

John and Barbara began by selecting one behavior, Tim's playing quietly while they had a conversation. They began to focus on when he did *not* interrupt rather than when he did interrupt. John, in particular, found this to be extremely difficult. His approach to handling any type of problem always had been to address it directly when it occurred rather than focusing on how to prevent the problem from occurring. Therefore, Barbara initially took the lead in working on Tim's interrupting behavior. Whenever John and Barbara engaged in a conversation, Barbara would turn to Tim and praise him for playing quietly. Initially, Tim looked at her in a puzzled manner and, on occasion, asked why she was talking like that to him.

Before long he would simply look at her, smile, and continue playing. As Barbara continued to praise Tim for not interrupting, John gradually began entering in with positive comments of his own to Tim. Tim's interruptions of his parents' conversations occurred less and less often, and with time the Smiths found they could praise less often than they did initially.

Once Barbara and John felt that they were focusing on the periods of time when Tim was not interrupting, they decided to begin rewarding a second positive behavior. By focusing on one behavior at a time and then moving to another behavior, the Smiths did not feel so overwhelmed by Tim's problem behaviors. Rather, they slowly but effectively addressed each of his behaviors that caused difficulties in the home. Not surprisingly, Barbara and John found that with each new behavior they addressed, it was easier for them to use rewards for good behavior, and Tim's behavior changed more rapidly.

Not only did Barbara and John begin rewarding Tim's good behavior, but they also began using the same skills with Susan. Her behavior improved even faster than did Tim's. Getting her to perform daily chores, like cleaning her room, required minimum effort by either Barbara or John once they explained clearly to Susan what they meant by a clean room and praised her during and after she cleaned it.

John and Barbara Smith felt they were on a roll. They had a plan and could see positive change in Tim's behavior occurring in small steps. Furthermore, they were on the way to a more pleasant family life, including a better relationship between the two of them. Working together to effectively solve problems had more payoffs than they had anticipated!

The Jones Family

When we last tuned in to Patricia and Lisa Jones, more positive times were occurring between the two of them as

Patricia used the attending skill. The concept of rewards came easily to Patricia, as she was receiving substantial attention in her career. Furthermore, the attention she received in her new dating relationship was a positive contrast to the lack of attention from Ed during their marriage. Thus, the idea of focusing on positive behavior, rewarding small changes in behavior, and using praise with Lisa made sense to her.

As with attending, what was difficult for Patricia was the time and energy to identify, focus on, and praise positive behaviors, which were rare. With the help of some problem solving with her friend and confidant at work, Patricia decided to set aside several hours twice a week to engage in an enjoyable activity without Lisa or anyone else. Patricia felt that this time would allow her to clear her head and focus more on Lisa's good behaviors. Patricia decided to resume horseback riding, an activity she had enjoyed before her marriage to Ed.

Patricia found horseback riding to be exactly what she needed. It was a time away from work and away from the daily hassles with Lisa. It allowed her to think about what particular behaviors of Lisa she wanted to try to increase and how to use rewards to achieve this goal. Furthermore, it gave her a renewed energy for this task. The new rule Patricia applied during horseback riding was not to think about work but rather to let her mind wander for a while and then to focus on Lisa.

Patricia experienced some guilt over taking time for herself when she was so busy and already had so little time with Lisa. However, her friend pointed out to her that she was simply applying the parenting program to herself—she was rewarding herself for a job well done with Lisa and allowing herself time to plan how to be a more effective parent for Lisa. Viewing her own behavior in this way, Patricia was able to control her guilty feelings. Besides, for the first time in a long time, she was happy with herself as a mother at home.

Common Concerns About Rewards

Like the Smiths, many parents have concerns about rewarding. Perhaps the most common question is "Isn't using rewards with my child just a way to bribe him?" In fact, bribery and rewards are *not* the same. We all work for rewards—just think about the rewards, including financial compensation, you receive for doing a good job at work. In contrast, bribery is used to induce someone to do something bad or wrong, which obviously is not our goal in using rewards with our children.

Some authorities maintain that praise is very different from encouragement. They view praise as being used only when a child accomplishes something and encouragement as being used for effort or improvement. These authorities further believe that praise is based on competition and comparison while encouragement is based on a child's assets and strengths. We disagree with this narrow view of praise. In our opinion, *praise* is used for effort and improvement and is *based on* a child's assets and strengths! We believe that many of the examples these authorities give of encouraging statements such as "You really worked hard on that" can also be viewed as a form of praise. In short, we believe that the distinction between encouragement and praise is often arbitrary and semantic. Praise and encouragement are both social rewards used to increase desirable behavior. All social rewards, including praise and encouragement, are important. We encourage you to use encouragement with your child!

Another common concern about rewards is whether the child will depend on the rewards and have no self-motivation. In fact, rewards don't destroy self-motivation, they actually enhance it. The way we—as parents, teachers, or supervisors—teach any new behavior is initially through rewards. Once the behavior is learned, we gradually decrease the external rewards, and self-rewards (self-motivation) take over to maintain the behavior. Thus, your rewards teach your strong-willed child what behaviors you, as a parent, want to see occur more frequently. With time and an improved relationship between the two of you, he will perform these behaviors to please you and himself.

Finally, many parents' experiences lead them to doubt the usefulness of rewards. Parents say, "I try to be as positive with my child as I can. I already have tried all those rewards, and my child's behavior is still terrible." True, most parents have made such attempts. But when rewards don't work, it is often because the parents have not learned and applied the principles of how to reward effectively. This chapter summarizes those principles and outlines a way to learn to use them.

How to Use Rewards Effectively

You can address the common concerns people have about rewards by using rewards effectively. To do this, follow these three important principles:

1. Use rewards immediately after the behavior you want to increase.
2. Initially reward the behavior every time it occurs.
3. Reward only behaviors you want to increase.

You really cannot wait until later in the evening to let your child know that you appreciated his coming into the house in the afternoon when you called him. Effective rewards occur immediately after the behavior you want to increase. Consequently, you need to be available and ready to praise your child *immediately* when he displays behavior you wish to increase.

Initially it is also important to praise a behavior, or even the approximation of a behavior, every time it occurs. This sounds like a big job, and it is. However, consistent rewards "prime the pump" and get good behavior started. As time passes, self-motivation increases, and you can reward the behavior less often.

Reward only the behaviors you want to increase. Rewarding behaviors you want to increase and ignoring behaviors you want to decrease will clearly show your child which behaviors you want to occur and which behaviors you do not want to occur. This is very important. The primary purpose of praising good behavior is to let your child know that this is the behavior you want to occur. If you also acknowledge bad behavior, the child will not learn what you are trying to teach. Your strong-willed child may be one who has learned that, in order to get attention, he has to behave badly. This principle of rewarding reverses the situation so that he gets attention when he is good and is ignored when he is bad. In the next chapter, we will present how to effectively ignore. For now, focus on rewarding behaviors you want to increase. Remember, in the five-week program you learn one skill at a time!

Learning to Use Rewards

Let's talk about how to begin using rewarding skills. First, in the two ten-minute practice sessions you have each day, continue attending and begin rewarding. If you used a tape recorder to record your attending sessions, continue to do this and listen to how you interact with your child. In particular, keep track of how many rewards you give. If your spouse or someone else can observe the sessions, as might have been done with attends, this also would be helpful. Either way, you need to receive feedback to make sure you are practicing this skill correctly. Many of us think we use these skills correctly and frequently; however, when we receive some objective feedback, we are shocked at how we are interacting. Remember, even if you

Guidelines for Practice Sessions: *Attending and Rewarding*	*TABLE 6-2*

Do Not	Do
Issue any instructions	Attend to (describe) your child's appropriate behavior
Ask any questions	Imitate your child's play behavior
	Verbally reward your child's appropriate behavior by praising him and labeling the desired behavior (e.g., "Thank you for picking up your toys!")
	Tape-record the session or have someone observe the session
	Evaluate your performance
	Reward yourself for your efforts and performance

are shocked, you should focus on what you did right. Apply your rewarding skills to yourself! The guidelines for the rewarding practice sessions are summarized in Table 6-2.

For the first three days, include rewards in your daily practice sessions. On the third day, also take a ten-minute private time by yourself or with your spouse. During this time think about three of your child's behaviors you would like to increase. This is an important point. Many people who seek help in parenting a strong-willed child are focused on finding out ways to decrease behaviors they do not like. At this point you should instead focus on behaviors to *increase.* For example, instead of thinking about ways to stop your strong-willed child from interrupting you and your spouse when the two of you are talking, think about ways to encourage your child to play quietly while you talk. Thus, the focus shifts from not interrupting to playing quietly, from disciplining your child for interrupting to rewarding him for playing quietly. The skills of

Focus on the Positive

You can benefit most from the powerful impact of praise if you concentrate on identifying the behaviors you want more of. For example, focus on sharing, not on snatching:

- Negative Behavior: "Stop grabbing toys from your sister."
- Positive Behavior: "While I was on the phone, I saw you share the toys with your sister. That was great!"

Focus on obedience, not on defiance:

- Negative Behavior: "Why are you being so disobedient?"
- Positive Behavior: "You put your shoes on so quickly when I asked!"

Focus on appropriate behavior, not on wild behavior:

- Negative Behavior: "I wish you would stop running through the aisles of the grocery store."
- Positive Behavior: "I'm pleased that you stayed by my side almost the whole time we were in the grocery store."

Focus on cooperation, not on tantrums:

- Negative Behavior: "Your crying every time I ask you to get out of your bath is driving me crazy."
- Positive Behavior: "Thank you for getting out of the bathtub quietly when I told you to get out."

rewarding and attending support your efforts to increase the positive behavior of your strong-willed child. Together, they help you find alternatives to punishing undesirable behavior.

During your ten-minute private time, eliminate all distractions, including television, radio, and noisy children. Identify three behaviors of your child that you want to increase. These behaviors should be relatively simple ones that occur almost daily. If you find yourself thinking about behaviors you want to decrease, turn them around and look at the positive side of those behaviors. Instead of focusing on your child ignoring directions, focus on when he does follow directions. Instead of focusing on inappropriate forms of persistence such as stubbornness, focus on appropriate forms of persistence such as continuing to work on a difficult puzzle.

Once you have identified the three behaviors, pick one of them. Ideally, you should pick the one you feel most able to change. That way you will be rewarded when your child's behavior changes. Next think about how you can use attends and rewards to increase that behavior. Examples of some behaviors to increase and the ways parents chose to increase them are presented in Table 6-3. Reading these might stimulate your thoughts and help you to see various ways to increase your child's positive behavior. Notice that you need to think through each situation and set the stage for appropriate behavior to occur. You cannot just wait for the desirable behavior to occur and then praise it. You need to develop a plan, focus on your child's positive behavior, and praise the behavior as soon as it occurs.

When you have selected the behavior and decided what you are going to do, the next step is to *do it*! Over the next few days, begin using attends and rewards to reinforce the behavior you selected. When you have seen an improvement, select a second behavior from the three you wanted to change and begin working on it. Several days later, even as you move into the next week of the program and the next skill, begin working on the third behavior. Continue to work on all three behaviors that you picked. In fact, you will probably *always* want to think about your child's behavior and decide whether there are behaviors you want to increase. When we say *always*, we mean literally until your child leaves home to take a job or go to college! As a parent of a young child, this may surprise you; however, we can assure you that there always will be some behavior you would like to see improve. As your child grows, the behaviors will change. What is reinforcing to him may change, but your focus on increasing positive behaviors should never change.

Your last assignment, which you should begin on day 5, is to start thinking about how you can use rewards

| ***Desirable Child Behaviors and Ways to Increase Them*** | **TABLE 6-3** |

Behaviors	*Suggested Procedure for Increasing Behavior*
Coming when called	1. Tell your child you want to work on improving his behavior when you call him. 2. Tell him exactly what you expect (for example, "When I call you, I expect you to stop what you are doing and come"). 3. Praise your child as soon as he comes in response to your call. 4. Praise him every time.
Staying with you in the grocery store	1. Put your child in a shopping cart so he will stay with you. On the first trip, praise and attend to him every 30 seconds. 2. On the next few trips, let him walk beside you as you hold his hand. Praise and attend to him every 30 seconds. 3. On the next few trips, lightly rest your hand on your child's shoulder. Praise and attend to him every 30 seconds. 4. On later trips, have your child walk beside you with no physical contact. Praise and attend to him every 30 seconds. 5. Gradually lengthen the time between your praise and attending statements, but never phase them out completely.
Playing cooperatively with sibling	1. Make your expectations clear (for example, "I want you two to play together without arguing or fighting"). 2. Monitor closely the play between the two children. 3. Praise appropriate play behavior.

throughout the day with your strong-willed child. Again, this involves focusing on your child's positive behaviors rather than on his negative behaviors. All children demonstrate some positive behavior, and that is what we want to praise. When we experience difficulties with a child, most of us reach a point where we can see only the negative aspects of his behavior. If you have reached this point, you will have to program focusing on the positive into your daily interactions with your child. This can be difficult at times. However, by focusing on the positive behaviors of your child, even if there are very few of them, you can begin to improve your interaction and relationship with your child.

There are countless situations in which you can use rewards with your child. Here are just a few examples to stimulate your thoughts about routine situations in which you may use rewards:

- Riding in the car
- Watching television
- Preparing dinner
- Eating dinner
- Bathing your child
- Grocery shopping together
- Dressing in the morning
- Working in the yard
- Washing dishes
- Putting your child to bed
- Waking your child in the morning
- Playing games together

Worksheet 6-1 outlines the assignments you need to complete during the second week of the five-week program. When you have completed these assignments, you will be ready to move to the next skill.

Daily Assignments for Week 2: Rewards | WORKSHEET 6-1

Tasks	1	2	3	4	5	6	7
Days							
1. Two 10-minute practice times	☐	☐	☐	☐	☐	☐	☐
2. Selection of 3 behaviors to increase		☐					
3. Increase first of 3 behaviors			☐	☐	☐	☐	☐
4. Consider use of rewards throughout day					☐	☐	☐
5. Increase second of 3 behaviors						☐	☐
6. Increase third of 3 behaviors			(week 3)				

7

Week 3: Ignoring

As you begin week 3 of the five-week program, continue your practice sessions and work on the three behaviors you selected to increase in week 2. In addition, you will be adding a new skill to your parenting repertoire—one that will make the attending and rewarding skills even more effective. This skill is *ignoring*. It is used to decrease behaviors you want to occur less often. By attending to and rewarding desirable behaviors and ignoring certain undesirable behaviors, you will make it clear to your strong-willed child which behaviors you want to see increase and which you want to decrease.

Appropriate Use of Ignoring

Ignoring is basically withholding attention from children. It has three primary components:

1. *No physical contact.* Do not touch your child.
2. *No verbal contact.* Do not talk to your child.
3. *No eye contact.* Do not look at your child.

Obviously, you have to respond if a child does something dangerous or destructive. You can't ignore behaviors like hitting, running in the street, or not following your instructions. We will talk about how to deal with these behaviors in Chapter 9. However, child behaviors that *can* be ignored include whining, tantrums, inappropriately demanding attention, and inappropriately crying.

For ignoring to work, you need to remove *all attention* from your child's behavior. This means you should not look at him, touch him, or talk to him. You should act as if you cannot see or hear him. You might even need to leave the room! Many parents have to leave when their child is having a tantrum or acting inappropriately. They go into a separate room in order to calm themselves.

What Behaviors *Can You* Ignore?

Children sometimes engage in behavior that is annoying or bad-mannered but that does not pose a danger to anyone or damage anything. The best way to decrease that kind of behavior is simply to ignore the child when it occurs. Here are some examples of behavior that usually meets the criteria for ignoring:

- Inappropriately demanding attention
- Demanding you do something you do not want to do
- Crying for attention
- Tantrums
- Screaming
- Pouting
- Showing off
- Arguing
- Acting irritable

Once you start ignoring a certain behavior, you must keep ignoring it. If you don't, your strong-willed child will learn that he can get your attention if he throws a tantrum or whines long enough. Unfortunately, what normally happens is that when you first start ignoring a bad behavior, it actually gets worse! This happens because children sometimes think that they are not acting bad enough to get your attention. However, if you continue ignoring the behavior, it is likely to decrease. If it does, the decrease is often fairly permanent, unless you start paying attention to the behavior again. Remember, attention can be physical contact, eye contact, or making some kind of comment.

To summarize, here are the basic principles of effective ignoring:

- Select a behavior that can be ignored.
- Remove all of your attention from the behavior when it occurs.
- Once you start ignoring a behavior, keep ignoring it.
- Expect the behavior to occur more often before it occurs less often.
- Reward and attend to appropriate behavior.

Think about how clear the message will be to your strong willed child if you attend to and praise him for playing appropriately with his toys and remove all of your attention when he screams and cries. He receives attention for playing appropriately and no attention for acting inappropriately. Under these conditions, it will not take long for him to learn what behaviors you want to see!

From the parents' standpoint, however, ignoring may be the *most difficult* skill to use. One reason is that inappropriate behavior may increase initially before subsiding. This is hard for parents to take! Furthermore, almost all of us as parents want to take some kind of immediate action whenever our strong-willed child is behaving inappropriately. We feel we must respond in order to change our child's behavior or to show that we are good parents. In contrast, ignoring the behavior basically involves doing nothing. This is difficult! So don't feel bad if you have to remove yourself from the situation in order to force yourself to "do nothing." You might go into the bathroom, close the door, and sit down for five minutes in order to gain control over yourself and not respond to your child's inappropriate behavior. However, you should remove yourself only if you are sure of your child's safety in your absence.

The Smith and Jones Families

Let's rejoin the Smith and Jones families and see what challenges and successes they experienced in learning the ignoring skill.

The Smith Family

When we last tuned in to the Smiths, Barbara and John were helping each other focus on Tim's positive behaviors. The next skill, ignoring undesirable behaviors such as disrupting their conversations, made logical sense. If attention is what a child wants, provide him with attention during the times when he is behaving appropriately and ignore his behavior at other times. Such an approach would make clear to Tim which behaviors are acceptable and unacceptable. However, using ignoring was no easy task for either of the Smiths.

John, in particular, found it very difficult to ignore disruptive behaviors. His idea was to address these behaviors straight on with some act of discipline; however, he recognized that the program thus far was quite effective, and his previous efforts at eliminating problem behavior had certainly not been effective. Thus, once again, he was willing to try out the new skill. To help John, the Smiths developed a plan. Whenever Tim's behavior, such as throwing a tantrum and demanding attention, became so aversive that John felt he had to respond, he would remove himself to the bathroom and remain there for five minutes. This ensured that he did not respond and Tim received no attention. Furthermore, during his practice times with Tim, Barbara would help John ignore inappropriate behavior by reminding him what to do and encouraging him to breath deeply and think about something pleasant.

With the use of rewards for appropriate behavior and ignoring for inappropriate behaviors such as interrupting, crying, demanding attention, and throwing temper tantrums, Tim's behavior began to change slowly across the days and weeks. Also, he seemed more content with himself and better able to control his emotions. His sister, Susan, even commented, "I don't mind Tim coming into my room sometimes now." The Smiths were making progress!

The Jones Family

When we last tuned into the Jones family, Patricia had decided to use horseback riding as a time to clear her head and decide how to spend time focusing on Lisa's behaviors. As with the Smiths, the notion of ignoring made sense; however, Patricia found it particularly difficult to ignore Lisa's tantrums. She felt she had very little time to spend with Lisa and, as a result, wanted there to be as little negative behavior as possible during these times. Rather than ignoring, Patricia was inclined to provide Lisa with attention or whatever else would terminate her tantrums.

Patricia decided to work on ignoring one behavior at a time. Lisa often demanded attention from her mother and then had a tantrum if she did not receive it when Patricia was involved in other activities. Patricia selected this behavior to ignore. During one of her horseback-riding sessions, Patricia tried to figure out ways to prevent demanding attention and tantrums from occurring, thus reducing how often she would need to ignore such behaviors (because they would occur less often). Patricia decided that spending more time with Lisa and focusing on her appropriate behaviors would leave less opportunity for the problem behaviors to occur. Furthermore, spending time with Lisa was actually enjoyable now.

Of course, Patricia knew she could not spend all of her free time with Lisa. She also knew this would not be healthy for either Lisa or herself. Thus, Patricia realized that she would need to use ignoring on at least some occasions. However, when tantrums did occur, Patricia did not feel as bad about ignoring Lisa because of the positive nature of their relationship at other times.

For Patricia, the tantrums that occurred in public places, like the grocery store, were the most difficult to ignore, primarily because they were so embarrassing. Patricia knew ignoring was the correct thing to do, but she worried about what others would think of her as a parent. Patricia finally resolved to "do what is correct." She increased her attention for appropriate behaviors, ignored tantrums, and ignored other people by turning her back and pretending to be closely examining the products on the shelf. It was not easy, but Lisa's tantrums gradually diminished, proving to Patricia that she had chosen the best course of action.

Learning the Ignoring Skills

During this week, your first assignment, beginning on day 1, is to incorporate ignoring skills into your practice sessions with your child. Combine ignoring with rewarding and attending. Praise appropriate behaviors and ignore certain inappropriate behaviors, such as tantrums, whining, and inappropriate demands for attention. Thus, in your practice sessions, if your strong-willed child demonstrates undesirable behaviors you can ignore, remove all attention by turning your back and saying nothing to him until his undesirable behavior totally stops. It may seem like forever; however, your actions will be a clear signal to him that you will not be attending to such behavior. Once the undesirable behavior stops, immediately turn back to your child and begin attending to and rewarding his appropriate behavior. Guidelines for practice sessions during week 3 are presented in Table 7-1.

The second assignment, beginning on day 2, is to pick out a behavior you feel you can ignore outside the practice sessions. This should be a behavior that occurs almost daily, such as those we have mentioned earlier in this

Guidelines for Practice Sessions: Attending, Rewarding, and Ignoring	TABLE 7-1

Do Not	Do
Issue any instructions	Attend to (describe) your child's appropriate behavior
Ask any questions	
	Imitate your child's play behavior
	Verbally reward your child's appropriate behavior by praising him and labeling the desired behavior (e.g., "Thank you for picking up your toys!")
	Ignore inappropriate behavior
	Tape-record the session or have someone observe the session
	Evaluate your performance
	Reward yourself for your efforts and performance

chapter. When you have selected a behavior, sit down with your strong-willed child and explain that the behavior is unacceptable, you will ignore it, *and* you will give attention for appropriate behavior. Do everything you can to make it clear to your child which behaviors you want to occur and which you do not want to occur. Here is how one mother explained to her child a behavior she would be ignoring:

> "Johnny, you know how we have been working on how you and I get along with each other. We have been spending lots of time together, and I try to say lots of positive things when you are behaving well. Well, we are going to work on some different things now. You know how when I say, "No, you can't have a cookie," you sometimes scream and cry. Well, two things are going to happen. First, when I say, "No,

you can't have a cookie," I really mean that you cannot have a cookie. Do you understand? Second, if you scream and cry, I am going to just walk away from you and not say anything to you. This is my way of saying that I don't like you screaming and crying when I say you can't have a cookie. When you don't scream and cry, I will be sure to let you know how proud of you I am. Do you have any questions?"

Begin ignoring the selected behavior on day 2. You will need to work carefully to make sure you totally ignore this behavior.

On day 5 select a second behavior to ignore. Follow the same procedure as before to explain what you will be ignoring, then begin ignoring the behavior.

Using Worksheet 7-1, list the behaviors you want to decrease by ignoring. Then indicate your success in ignoring undesirable behaviors. If you successfully ignored the behavior during the day, place a check in the box for that day. Remember, this process will take time, and it will not be easy! Also, remember that, for ignoring of tantrums and other similar behaviors to be effective, you also will need to praise appropriate behavior. Ignoring inappropriate behavior is effective only within the context of attending to and rewarding appropriate behavior.

Charting Your Success in Ignoring Inappropriate Behavior	**WORKSHEET 7-1**					
				Days		
Behaviors to Ignore	2	3	4	5	6	7
1.	☐	☐	☐	☐	☐	☐
2.				☐	☐	☐

Worksheet 7-2 outlines the assignments to be completed during the third week of the program. After you have followed these steps, you will be ready to move to the next skill.

Daily Assignments for Week 3: Ignoring	**WORKSHEET 7-2**						
				Days			
Tasks	1	2	3	4	5	6	7
1. Two 10-minute practice times	☐	☐	☐	☐	☐	☐	☐
2. Ignoring first inappropriate behavior							
Select behavior		☐					
Explain to child		☐					
Ignore behavior		☐	☐	☐	☐	☐	☐
2. Ignoring second inappropriate behavior							
Select behavior					☐		
Explain to child					☐		
Ignore behavior					☐	☐	☐

8

Week 4: Giving Directions

By this time in the program, you may have begun to notice changes in your strong-willed child's behavior. In particular, you may find that being with him is more pleasant and many of the interactions you have with him are less stressful than in the past. If so, then you are well on your way to a better relationship with your child!

The first three weeks of the program focused primarily on ways to improve your strong-willed child's behavior through changing your attention. By increasing positive attention toward your child, particularly when he is behaving appropriately, you increase the odds he will cooperate with you and comply when you give directions. Those skills bring you to the phase where you can work directly on compliance. To do this, you must cultivate your skill in giving directions.

Keeping Directions Clear

In our clinical work with parents of strong-willed children, we have observed that parents often give instructions their child cannot easily comply with. The parents may give too many directions at one time, give vague directions, or actually distract their child from complying.

TABLE 8-1

Ineffective Directions

Type of Directions	Definition	Likely Consequences
Chain direction	Direction that involves numerous steps.	Your young child may not be able to remember all the things you told him to do. Therefore, he may not follow such a direction.
Vague direction	Direction that is not clear and may be interpreted by your child in a different way than you intended. For example, "Be good" can mean different things in different situations.	Your child may not be able to correctly interpret and follow the direction. Being "good" in one situation may mean staying seated at the table; in another situation, it may mean not hitting his sibling.
Question direction	Direction in the form of a question, which gives your child the option of saying "no."	Asking your child to do something may sound less authoritarian, but it places you in the position of having to accept "no" as an answer.
Direction followed by a reason	Reason given after a direction.	A reason after a direction can distract a young child from complying. If you want to use a reason, keep it short and give the reason before you give the direction.

They then become frustrated and angry with their child, even though he really did not have a chance to comply. To avoid such problems with your child, you need to give clear and simple directions.

One way to recognize clear directions is to compare them with types of directions you do *not* want to use with your child. These are chain directions, vague directions, question directions, and directions followed by a reason (see Table 8-1). Each type of ineffective direction makes it difficult for your strong-willed child to comply—just the opposite of what you want to happen.

Chain Directions

A *chain direction* consists of giving several directions at one time. For example, if you say, "Get dressed, brush your teeth, comb your hair, and come downstairs for breakfast," you are actually telling your child to do four different things. The problem with a chain direction is that your young child may not have the cognitive abilities to process this much information and remember all parts of the direction. Therefore, if you give a chain direction to your young strong-willed child, he may be unable to comply even if he wants to do so! You will have set up a situation where noncompliance has to occur and you have not been fair to your child.

An effective alternative to giving a chain direction is to break the direction down into smaller steps and give each part of it individually. For example, first tell your child to brush his teeth. When he has brushed his teeth, praise him and tell him to comb his hair. When he has combed his hair, use your rewarding skills to let him know you appreciate his following your direction. By issuing directions individually, rather than in a chain, you increase the chances of your child's complying.

Vague Directions

Children also have difficulty with *vague directions*—directions that are not clear or specific. Examples include "Be good," "Act nice," and "Behave like you should." The problem with this kind of instruction is that your child may not know what you actually want him to do. What you mean and what he thinks you mean might be very different!

It is much better to state directly what you want him to do. "Share your toys with your brother" is a better direction than "Play nicely" or "Be good when you play together." The more specific you are, the more likely your child is to follow your directions.

Question Directions

Question directions ask your child whether he will do something, rather than directing him to do so. For example, "Would you like to clean your room now?" is not a clear direction. It creates a problem because your strong-willed child can—and probably will—simply say no. If your intent is to give a direction to your child and have him follow it, you should not phrase it in the form of a question and allow him the option of refusing. When a child says "no" to a question direction, many parents become upset with their child for being defiant. However, the parents are really responsible for giving their child the option of refusing.

Instead of using question directions carelessly, consider first whether you really want to give your child the option of whether to comply. Asking, "Would you like to clean your room now?" is acceptable if you want to give your child the option of cleaning his room now or later. However, this is not what most parents mean when they use directions in the form of a question. Unless you really mean for your child to have the option, avoid this type of direction.

It is, however, important to give young children frequent options and choices, so they can learn how to make decisions. For example, from an early age children should be given choices such as what book they want you to read at bedtime, what clothes they want to wear, and within reason what they want to eat for a snack. However, it also is important to limit the choices of young children, so that they are not overwhelmed by the options. Asking, "Do you want to wear your red or blue shirt today?" is easier for a young child to handle than, "What do you want to wear today?" You want to give your child choices; however, be careful not to confuse questions and directions.

Directions Followed by a Reason

The last type of ineffective direction is one that is *followed by a reason*. An example is "Pick up your toys because your grandmother is coming over, and you know how she likes a clean house." The problem with this type of direction is that your child may forget the original direction or be distracted by the reason that followed it. Remember, a young child's cognitive abilities are not developed well enough to retain the same amount of information that adults can. Giving a reason or explanation after you have issued the instruction may distract your strong-willed child or cause him to forget what you originally asked him to do. As a result, he will fail to follow your direction.

Giving a short reason or an explanation for a particular instruction is certainly appropriate, however. The effective way to do so is to give the reason first. Returning to the previous example, the parent might change the order of the direction and the reason in the following way: "Grandmother is coming over, and she likes a clean house, so please pick up your toys now." In this way, the direction is the last thing you say and the last thing your child hears. A child is more likely to comply with this direction than one where the reason follows the request.

| *Identifying Effective and* | **WORKSHEET 8-1** |
| *Ineffective Directions* | |

Place a check next to each statement that is an effective direction. What makes each of the remaining directions ineffective?

☐ 1. "Johnny, hand me the red block."

☐ 2. "Why don't we play the card game now?"

☐ 3. "Please be careful."

☐ 4. "Please sit beside me."

☐ 5. "Put the red block here, and then put the green block over there."

☐ 6. "Johnny, you really need to be good when we play together."

☐ 7. "Because I want you to build a high tower, put the red block on top of the blue block."

☐ 8. "Put the red block on top of the blue block because I want you to build a high tower."

☐ 9. "Would you like to clean up now?"

☐ 10. "Please clean up, put on your coat, and go outside."

Answers: Numbers 1, 4, and 7 are effective directions. Numbers 2 and 9 are ineffective because they are questions. Numbers 3 and 6 are vague. Numbers 5 and 10 are chain directions. Number 8 is a direction followed by a reason.

To check whether you can already recognize different types of directions, use Worksheet 8-1. Read each direction and decide whether it is effective or ineffective. Place a check in the box next to each effective direction. If you believe the direction is ineffective, write whether it is a chain direction, vague direction, question direction, or direction followed by a reason. Then compare your answers with the ones at the bottom of the worksheet. If you got at least eight answers correct, you have a good grasp of what makes directions effective.

The Smith and Jones Families

Let's rejoin the Smith and Jones families and see what they discovered about the way they give directions. As they learned to issue effective directions, they faced a variety of challenges but enjoyed successes as well.

The Smith Family

When we last tuned in to the Smith family, John and Barbara had changed much of their daily routine with Tim. They now were having regular playtimes, focusing on positive behavior throughout the day, and ignoring some inappropriate behavior such as tantrums and demanding attention. However, some daily activities, such as picking up toys and taking a bath, still required the Smiths to issue instructions to Tim. Unfortunately, although Tim's relationship with each parent had improved and he did comply more than in the past, compliance with directions was still a problem.

The idea of issuing simple instructions to Tim one at a time made sense to the Smiths. However, Barbara and John found that they had to remind each other not to give chain commands and to give simple commands they were sure Tim could understand. John later said, "It was hard to think about giving straightforward directions to Tim. I think I've always been afraid to tell him directly to do something because I knew he probably would not comply. Then I'd get angry and end up feeling bad."

Once Barbara and John began focusing on how they gave directions to Tim, they learned to set the stage so that he complied much more often than in the past. That is, they began to think about which directions were most important for Tim to follow, and they issued only these, using a simple and straightforward manner. They also prepared Tim with warnings (for example, "In five minutes you'll begin cleaning up") and praised him as soon as he began showing signs of compliance. As they had with other skills, John and Barbara first focused on how they issued directions in only one problem situation—toy cleanup in the afternoon. Next, they addressed how they issued instructions for taking a bath. It was beginning to be almost easy—solving one problem at a time by using the combination of skills they were learning in the program.

The Jones Family

When we last visited the Jones family, Patricia was rewarding positive behavior and ignoring Lisa's inappropriate behavior. Although the positive times with Lisa had definitely increased, Patricia still had problems when she needed Lisa to do something immediately.

Patricia found the idea of simple and straightforward directions very beneficial. She had to focus on Lisa when she was giving instructions and had to think carefully about how she worded those instructions. When she began doing so, Lisa appeared more responsive. Patricia also discovered that many of the directions she was giving Lisa were really not important. Patricia found that she had given many directions in the hope Lisa would comply occasionally. Patricia began to think carefully before giving directions and decided whether each was important for Lisa to do. For those that were important, she then thought carefully about how to issue the direction in the form of a simple instruction. Because she often was pressed for time, Patricia also had to work hard to allow Lisa time to begin complying. However, one thing that did come easy was rewarding Lisa for compliance. This had become natural for Patricia!

In response to Patricia's simple and straightforward instructions coupled with rewards for compliance, Lisa's compliance in various problem situations improved substantially. However, by no stretch of the imagination was Lisa compliant most of the time.

Principles of Giving Directions

By avoiding chain directions, vague directions, question directions, and directions followed by a reason, you—like the Smiths and Patricia Jones—will enhance the likelihood that your strong-willed child will comply with the request you make. Effective directions will eliminate confusion for your child and increase the probability of compliance. So, exactly how should you give effective directions? These are the critical components of that process:

- Get your child's attention and make eye contact before giving a direction.
- Use a firm, but not loud or gruff, voice.
- Give a direction that is specific and simple.
- Use physical gestures when appropriate (such as pointing to where to put the toys).
- Use "do" directions rather than "don't" directions.
- Reward compliance.
- Think before giving a direction, and make sure you are willing to gain compliance regardless of the amount of time, energy, or effort required.

First, before giving a direction, make sure you have your child's attention. One way to ensure that you have his attention is to make eye contact with him *before* you actually issue the direction. To do this, you might say, "Johnny, I have something to say. Please look at me."

When giving a direction, use a firm voice. It should *not* be loud or gruff, but it needs to be firm. Practice using a firm voice with your spouse, in front of a mirror, or on a tape recorder. You may be surprised at how you sound. Many parents sound as if they are begging their child to comply, while others, through gritted teeth, sound like a sergeant in the military. Neither style represents the firm voice we are proposing you use.

Use a direction that is specific and simple. If possible, supplement your words with gestures such as pointing.

For example, point to the bathroom if you are telling your child to wash his face.

Whenever possible, use positive directions ("do this") instead of negative ones ("don't do this"). For example, when you and your strong-willed child are shopping together, you can say, "Stay by my side," instead of, "Don't run ahead of me." Using positive directions creates a better relationship with your child and a better learning situation. It also makes it easy to praise your child for following your direction.

Once your child complies, use those attending and rewarding skills you learned during weeks 1 and 2. This is a way to let your child know you appreciate his compliance. As we have stated repeatedly, praise will let your strong-willed child know which of his behaviors you want to see increase.

Finally, give only directions you are prepared to follow through on to gain compliance from your child. If your child does not follow your direction and you do nothing, what is going to happen? He will learn that you do not mean what you say, and his strong-willed behavior will increase. Thus, you need to be willing to follow through and use a consequence for noncompliance to your directions. (However, this is what you will learn in week 5 of the program. For this week, just focus on how to give effective instructions.)

How do these principles fit with the first week of the five-week program (Chapter 5) when you learned to use the attending skill? When you started working on attending, you also reduced the number of directions and questions you used with your child. As you did so, you may have realized that you primarily spoke to your child using directions and questions. But some situations do require giving directions, so we now focus on making sure that each direction is a "good direction" and that you work with your child to obtain compliance. In sum, children need fewer directions and questions than we usually direct toward them, but when you do tell your child to do something, you should make it a direction he can comply with *and* you should be willing to exert the effort needed to obtain compliance.

Learning to Give Directions Effectively

During the first three weeks of the five-week program, you set aside two ten-minute periods per day to practice attending, rewarding, and ignoring. Now you have the option of replacing one of these periods with a ten-minute session in which you practice giving good directions. However, you may choose to keep both ten-minute sessions for attending, rewarding, and ignoring and add a third ten-minute session to practice giving directions. The important point is that you must keep *at least* one ten-minute session for attending, rewarding, and ignoring.

In the direction-issuing session, tell your child that you will be deciding the rules of the session. You must make it clear that the rules of the session will be different from those of the sessions in which you practice attending, rewarding, and ignoring. Your child needs to know that it is not his playtime anymore; rather, you will be in charge. You might say, "We have been playing things you wanted to play. Now I am going to be in charge and decide what we will do." One thing he will learn from this is that sometimes it is his time to decide the rules and other times it is your time to decide the rules. Once you have established this, practice giving clear and simple directions to your child. If you want ideas for directions to give, you may want to look back to the Compliance Test in Chapter 4.

As you did during weeks 1 through 3, tape-record your session or have someone record your directions. In either case, use Worksheet 8-2 to count effective directions and

Record of Direction Giving	**WORKSHEET 8-2**						
Tally the number of each type of direction you issue each day during your practice session.							
	Days						
	1	2	3	4	5	6	7
Effective Directions	—	—	—	—	—	—	—
Ineffective Directions: Chain direction	—	—	—	—	—	—	—
Vague direction	—	—	—	—	—	—	—
Question direction	—	—	—	—	—	—	—
Direction followed by a reason	—	—	—	—	—	—	—
Total Number of Ineffective Directions	—	—	—	—	—	—	—

ineffective directions. Your goal is to give at least twenty directions in a ten-minute period and for at least four times as many directions to be effective as ineffective.

During this daily direction-giving session, praise your child for complying with your directions. If he does not comply, simply ignore him for five seconds and then issue another direction. As we indicated earlier, next week you will work on the consequences of not complying. For the time being, simply ignore noncompliance during the practice session.

On days 3 and 4, continue the same practice sessions and also pick out a daily activity that usually involves your giving directions to your child. This may be dressing for preschool or school in the morning, or it may be your evening routine of bathtime and preparing for bed. In whatever situation you choose, practice using simple, firm, clear directions. Give your child time to comply and reward him for complying. If he does not follow your directions, use whatever procedures you typically use.

On day 5, select another situation that involves giving directions to your child, and begin focusing on how you give directions in that situation. Doing this will help you integrate what you have practiced in the direction-giving sessions into your daily routine. As we have emphasized repeatedly, this will be necessary for your behavior to change and for your child's behavior to change. Giving good directions is an excellent way to promote behavior change!

Daily Assignments for Week 4: Directions		**WORKSHEET 8-3**						
		Days						
Tasks	*1*	*2*	*3*	*4*	*5*	*6*	*7*	
1. At least one 10-minute practice time for attending, rewarding, ignoring	☐	☐	☐	☐	☐	☐	☐	
2. One 10-minute practice time for issuing directions	☐	☐	☐	☐	☐	☐	☐	
3. Select first daily situation in which to issue effective directions			☐	☐	☐	☐	☐	
4. Select second daily situation in which to issue effective directions					☐	☐	☐	

Worksheet 8-3 summarizes your assignments for week 4. When you have followed these steps, you will be ready to move to the final week of the program.

9

Week 5: Time-Out

By now you have built a better relationship with your child. Furthermore, he is complying more often with your instructions, in part because of your improved relationship and in part because you are giving good directions and praising his compliance. However, your child still will fail to comply at times. As we indicated in Chapter 8, you must be willing to provide a consequence for noncompliance. In other words, your child needs to understand that he will experience a negative consequence for failure to comply, just as he experiences a positive consequence (praise) for compliance.

You must be willing to use the consequence *every time* your child fails to follow your direction. If you do, he will quickly learn that you are not going to ignore or give in to his noncompliance. Once your child realizes that you are going to consistently use a consequence for noncompliance, he will have no reason to constantly test the limits by not complying.

Many parents are inconsistent in responding to their child's noncompliance. For example, one day you may have responded to his refusal to take a bath by saying, "OK, just be dirty if you want to," whereas on another day you may have said, "You are going to take a bath now, and I mean it!" This inconsistency in your reaction promotes further noncompliance because your child never knows what you are going to do, and he may test the limits to see exactly what you will do on any given occasion. In contrast, consistently using a specific consequence eliminates much of your child's testing and the related failure to obey.

Remember the context in which your child's noncompliance is *now* occurring. You have reduced the number of directions you are giving; when you do issue them, they are clear and concise; and you are rewarding compliance. In this context, you probably will not have to apply consequences in most situations. This is evidence of the better relationship you now have with your child!

In our experience, most parents of strong-willed children have tried a variety of consequences for noncompliance and other problem behaviors. These consequences have ranged from ignoring to reasoning to threatening to spanking. All of these pose problems. While you can ignore attention-seeking behaviors such as whining or tantrums, you simply cannot ignore noncompliance or some other behaviors such as aggression or dangerous behaviors. If you ignore noncompliance or aggression, they will occur more frequently because they achieve their purpose and therefore are reinforced. For example, if you ignore noncompliance, your child learns that he can avoid doing what you tell him to do. As a result, his noncompliance will be negatively reinforced and will occur more frequently. In a similar fashion, aggression should not be ignored, not only because it is dangerous, but also because when ignored it will occur more frequently if it still achieves its goal, such as hurting the other person.

Reasoning is what most of us as parents would prefer to do. After all, if you could explain to your child why he should comply, wouldn't he do so? Unfortunately, reasoning rarely convinces strong-willed children. In fact, it does just the opposite: it rewards your child with your undivided attention for noncompliance! Threatening wild consequences ("You will never watch TV again as long as you live if you don't do what I say now!") will not work because your child knows you cannot carry them out (even if you want to sometimes). Spankings do more to vent parents' frustration and anger than to improve a child's behavior. In addition, spanking does not allow either parent or child to calm down, and it may teach a child that physical aggression is a way to solve a problem. This is not what you want your strong-willed child to learn!

The consequence that we recommend you use for non-compliance is *time-out*. This refers to putting your child in a boring place for several minutes and withholding attention from him. In contrast to most forms of punishment, which involve doing something aversive or painful to your child, time-out is the removal of the opportunity to receive any attention. That is, rather than being a typical form of punishment, it is the *removal* of positive consequences. This can be just as effective as most forms of punishment without the negative side effects that many punishment procedures have. In addition, as a result of the first part of the five-week program, your attention is now very important to your child, which will make time-out effective.

Effective Time-Out

Most parents have heard of time-out. Like many of the parents with whom we have worked, you may have even tried time-out and concluded that it is not effective. But once we have shown parents the correct way to use time-out, their child's behavior does change, and they realize that time-out does work. We think you will reach the same conclusion if you follow exactly our directions in this chapter. Research has demonstrated that these procedures are the most effective ways of implementing time-out. It is important to follow the procedures exactly as we present them. Minor changes can decrease the effectiveness of time-out significantly!

Choosing a Time-Out Location	TABLE 9-1
Best Options	• Hallway • Parents' bedroom • Kitchen corner (for two- and three-year-old children)
Least Desirable Option	• Child's bedroom
Not Options	• Bathroom • Closet • Dark room

First choose a location for time-out in your home. There are a number of things you need to consider in choosing this place. It should be away from toys, people, windows, televisions, radios, and anything else your child enjoys. Remember, time-out means your child is receiving no positive attention from you or anyone or anything else. Second, nothing breakable should be nearby. Why cause a disaster by putting your child in time-out next to a valuable lamp? Table 9-1 summarizes locations that are suitable and not suitable for time-out.

One good place for time-out is at the end of a hallway. This is typically a place away from people and other enjoyable activities (for example, watching television). If you use a hallway for a time-out area, we recommend keeping an adult-size chair in the time-out place. This can serve several useful purposes. First, it can remind your child that this is the time-out area. In addition, it helps you define where he should be during a time-out (that is, in the chair). Also, an adult-size chair will keep your child's feet off the floor, so he will be less likely to get up during time-out. Be careful not to put the chair so close to the wall that your child can continually kick the wall, perhaps putting a hole through it.

A bedroom is also a possible location. Your child's bedroom may contain too many enjoyable activities, however. If it does and you absolutely must use your child's bedroom as the time-out area, remove all toys from the room. Your own bedroom may be a preferable location because it probably contains fewer things to entertain your child. Just make sure there are no breakables in the room.

For children who are two or three years old, a corner in the kitchen may be a good option. You can keep an eye on your child while he is in time-out. Be sure, however, not to make any contact (visual, verbal, or physical) with him.

Some parents identify a bathroom as a time-out area. This can be dangerous if it contains medicine, razor blades, or other potentially harmful objects. Consequently, we do not recommend using a bathroom as a time-out area.

Whatever location you select, never turn off the lights as part of time-out. This will only scare your child. For the same reason, never use a closet or small enclosed area for time-out. The purpose of time-out is to remove your child temporarily from attention, not to frighten him.

The Time-Out Procedure

When you use time-out for your child's noncompliance, you need to follow an exact sequence for implementing the procedure. The steps to use are summarized in Table 9-2. When you have given a simple and clear direction, wait five seconds for your child to begin complying. If he does comply, praise him. If he does not, give one warning: "If you do not _____, you will have to take a time-out." Issue this warning in a matter-of-fact voice without yelling or becoming angry. Wait five seconds. If your child begins complying, praise him. If he does not, take him by the hand and say only, "Because you did not _____, you have to take a time-out." Say this only once and in a calm but firm voice. Do not lecture, scold, or argue with your child, and do not accept any excuses. Then lead your child by the hand to time-out. Do not talk to him while

Time-Out Sequence for Noncompliance	**TABLE 9-2**

1. Issue a good direction.
2. If your child does not begin to comply within 5 seconds, issue a warning: "If you do not _____, you will have to take a time-out."
3. If your child does not begin to comply within 5 seconds, state, "Because you did not _____, you have to take a time-out."
4. Lead your child to time-out without lecturing, scolding, or arguing.
5. Ignore shouting, protesting, and promising to comply.
6. Tell him to sit in the time-out chair.
7. When he is sitting quietly, set the timer for the appropriate length of time-out (1 minute for each year of age).
8. When his time is over, including being quiet for the last 30 seconds, return to the chair and tell him time-out is over.
9. Restate the original direction.
10. Implement the time-out again if your child does not comply.

leading him to the time-out chair. Ignore shouting, protesting, and promises to comply.

When you tell your child he has to take a time-out, his response may trigger one of two problems. First, he may immediately begin complying. If he does, do not give in but move ahead with implementing time-out. This is difficult because, after all, he did finally comply. However, think about what he will be learning: "I don't have to comply until my mom gives me a direction, a warning, and then starts to take me to time-out." Obviously, this is not your goal. Second, your child may resist going to time-out when you start to lead him to the chair. If this occurs, stand behind him, put your hands in his armpits, lift him up so he is facing away from you, take him to the time-out chair, and put him in the chair as you stand behind it.

When you and your child reach the time-out chair, tell him to sit down. When he is quiet, set a timer and tell him to stay in the chair until the timer sounds. Place the timer where he can see but not touch it. Set the timer for one minute for each year of his age. A three-year-old should have a three-minute time-out, and a five-year-old should have a five-minute time-out.

The length of the time-out should also depend on a requirement that your child be quiet before you end the time-out. There is nothing magical about the "one minute per year of age" rule. Young children are not very good at estimating whether they have been in time-out for two minutes or three minutes. When you first begin using time-out, require your child to be quiet for the last thirty seconds of time-out. If he is screaming or kicking the wall at the end of his time-out period, wait until he has been quiet for at least thirty seconds beyond the time-out period before removing him. After several weeks of using time-out, change the requirement so that your child has to be quiet for the last minute of time-out. Gradually continue to lengthen the time he has to be quiet before leaving time-out. This is important because your child will learn that good behavior in time-out is important and is required for leaving time-out. Do not end the time-out until your child is quiet!

After the time-out period is over, return to the chair and tell your child that he may get up. Since he had to go to time-out for not following a direction, return to the scene where he initially failed to comply, and give the original direction again. You must do this, or he will learn that he can get out of following your directions if he takes a time-out. If your child goes to time-out for refusing to pick up toys and you pick them up while he is in time-out, he will learn that he can avoid picking up his toys by taking a time-out. Once he is out of time-out and you have issued the direction again, follow the same sequence leading to time-out if he does not comply.

Consequences for Compliance and Noncompliance

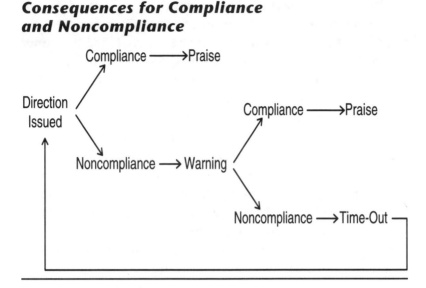

The flow chart at the top of this page shows the different consequences that you should apply depending on whether your child complies with your directions. Remember, after using time-out, you always return to issuing the direction again. Theoretically, you could stay in the sequence *forever* if your child never complied. However, we recommend that you continue this sequence only until your child complies or he reaches his eighteenth birthday (just kidding!). Seriously, you must stick with it until he complies, and he will when he becomes aware of your determination. As soon as he complies, praise him!

Some parents want to spend time discussing in detail with their child why time-out was used, their love for the child, and how horrible it made them feel to have to use time-out. Other parents want to have a discussion with their child in order to induce guilt over not complying and receive an apology from the child. Neither of these two types of discussions is desirable or helpful. A brief comment ("You had to go to time-out because you did not do what Mommy told you to do"), but no more, is acceptable after time-out.

Overcoming Time-Out Problems

You may encounter several problems when using time-out. One of the most common is that your child may not stay in the time-out chair when you tell him to do so. If this happens, you have several options. First, if he initially refuses to sit or stay in the chair, you can tell him that the time-out period will not even start until he sits down in the chair. A second option is that you can place him in the chair again, say, "Stay in the chair," and place your hand on his leg to encourage him to remain seated. A third option for a child who is five years of age or older is to tell him that, if he does not return to the time-out chair, he will lose a privilege. For example, you could say in a calm voice, "If you get up again, you can't ride your bike the rest of the day." Remember, if you say it, do it! Removing privileges will not work with children under five because they have difficulty bridging the gap in time between what is happening now and enjoying the privilege later.

Another common problem is that your child may say things in time-out that are painful for you to hear. Here are some of the most common statements that upset parents:

- "I have to go to the potty."
- "I don't love you anymore."
- "I'm going to run away."
- "I hate you."
- "I like time-out better than being with you."
- "You are ugly and mean."
- "I wish I was dead."
- "I am going to call 911."
- "I wish you were not my mommy."
- "I wish you were not my daddy."

You just have to ignore these statements!

Some parents report that while their child sits in the chair, he pushes the chair slowly out of the time-out area with his feet. This is one reason for using an adult-size chair in time-out. With such a chair, your child's feet can't touch the floor. Therefore, if he does push the chair out of the time-out area, he has to be out of the chair. In that case, follow through with one of the three options we presented for handling a child who leaves time-out.

Sometimes a child refuses to come out of time-out when it is over. If this occurs, you need to take control and tell him that you are imposing another time-out period. After all, refusing to leave time-out is another case of not complying. Set the timer again. When the timer goes off, return to the time-out area and again tell him that he should leave time-out. If he still refuses to come out of time-out, start the timer again. Do this until your child agrees to come out and follow the instruction you originally issued. He will eventually agree!

Table 9-3 summarizes these and other time-out problems and solutions. Time-out is a complicated procedure, so you will need to practice it before using it with your child. Toward the end of this chapter, we will spell out how to learn, practice, and use time-out for noncompliance.

Using Time-Out for Other Problems

The time-out procedure you will learn can be used not only to handle noncompliance but also with other behavior problems. Continue to ignore behaviors that you identified in week 3, such as crying, tantrums, and demands for attention. However, noncompliance is only one of the negative behaviors you cannot ignore. You need to respond when your child does any of these things:

- Hitting a sibling, playmate, or parent
- Running into the street
- Jumping on furniture

Time-Out Problems and Possible Solutions	**TABLE 9-3**

Problem	Possible Solutions
Refusing to sit in the chair	• Do not start time-out until he is seated.
Leaving or moving the chair	• Stop the timer until he sits down. • Place him in the chair, tell him to stay, and place your hand on his leg. • Remove a privilege if he does not return to the chair (for 5-year-olds and up).
Insulting you verbally	• Ignore the insults.
Yelling and crying	• Ignore the yelling and crying.
Refusing to leave time-out	• Start time-out over.
Sibling interacting with child while he is in time-out	• Put the sibling in time-out in another location.

- Biting another child
- Destroying household objects or toys of another child
- Using bad language
- Talking back to a parent or another adult
- Kicking, slapping, pinching, or hair pulling
- Throwing objects that are not meant to be thrown

The most effective response to these behaviors is a time-out procedure similar to the one presented for noncompliance. However, the procedure will differ in several ways. First, tell your child only one time not to engage in any of these behaviors. Tell him that, if he does the behavior, time-out will immediately occur. Also, because these behaviors do not involve you giving him an initial direction, state your expectations by preparing a list of House Rules. If your child violates a House Rule, never issue a warning. Instead, use time-out immediately.

Explaining House Rules: An Example

Here is how one mother explained House Rules to her four-year-old:

"Johnny, let's turn off the TV and talk for a few minutes. You know I have been getting upset with you sometimes around the house. I have really tried to praise you more and spend more time with you. I also am going to set up some House Rules to help you behave better.

"House Rules are rules that you *always* should obey. If you don't obey a House Rule, you will have to immediately take a time-out. If you break a House Rule, I will tell you what you did, take you by the hand, lead you to time-out, and have you sit in time-out for four minutes. Let's practice going to time-out after breaking a House Rule. [Practice the procedure just described.]

"Now, see this piece of paper. On the top is written House Rules. I am going to write down three rules and put some pictures to show what you can and cannot do.

1. No jumping on furniture.
2. No hitting your sister.
3. No running in the house.

"Anytime you jump on the furniture, hit your sister, or run in the house, what will happen? That's right, you immediately will have to go to time-out.

"Now I am going to put the list here on the refrigerator. Every morning I will remind you of the rules.

"OK, now that we have set up some rules, let's go outside and toss your ball."

Depending on your own child's age, adapt this approach to the rules and needs of your own household.

Tell your child in advance which behaviors will result in immediate time-out. Prepare for this by listing your House Rules and posting them on the refrigerator or some other location where your child can see them. For young children who cannot read, present the rules in the form of pictures. Read the rules to your child, and review the time-out procedure for breaking the rules. Show him the time-out chair. Walk him through what will happen when he displays any of the behaviors. Have him repeat the list of behaviors and the procedure to make sure that he comprehends them. By making sure he understands what behaviors are acceptable and unacceptable and what will happen when the House Rules are broken, you are being fair to him. Also, remind him each day about the House Rules.

At the end of a time-out for breaking one of the House Rules, say, "You had to go to time-out because you broke a House Rule. Which rule did you break?" If he responds correctly, say, "That's right. Don't _____ again." If he responds incorrectly or does not respond, briefly tell him what rule he broke. Next, immediately try to involve your child in an activity (such as helping you do a task) so you can praise him.

You can also use time-out for noncompliance and other problem behaviors outside of the home. However, use it in public places only after you have successfully used it at home. The main difference in using time-out outside the home is that you have to identify an appropriate location. If you are shopping, you can use a corner of the store or the backseat of your car. If your child becomes disruptive, you can give him a warning: "If you do not keep your hands inside the shopping cart, you will take a time-out in the car." If your child does not comply, take him by the hand and lead him from the store. Place him in the backseat of your car and turn your back while standing outside the car. Make sure you have the keys to the car! Leave him in the car for the length of his time-out, then open the door and take him back into the store. Reinforce him as soon as he is behaving. When you use your car as a time-out, never leave your child alone.

The Smith and Jones Families

Time-out helped the Smith and Jones families manage noncompliance and other problem behaviors. Read on to find out how.

The Smith Family

When we last visited the Smith family, Tim's relationship with each parent had continued to improve. Furthermore, as his parents issued directions in a simple and straightforward manner, Tim's compliance was improving. However, he sometimes said he would comply ("I will pick up my toys in a minute") but didn't do so. At other times he refused to comply ("No, I don't want to pick up my toys!") or even threw a tantrum rather than comply. Barbara and John therefore welcomed the chance to use the time-out skill.

In the past, Tim's parents had handled his problem behaviors such as noncompliance with a variety of consequences. These consequences had included pleading, threatening, screaming, and, on some occasions, spanking. Neither Barbara nor John had found any of these consequences to be effective. Switching from one type of discipline to another in order to "make the punishment fit the crime" just had not worked. Furthermore, Barbara and John usually felt bad after screaming, threatening, or spanking. So the Smiths liked the idea of using time-out for every act of noncompliance and for other behaviors that could not be ignored.

Tim was a creative child. When his parents began using time-out, he pushed every limit. He moved the time-out chair around the room without actually leaving the chair, refused to get out of time-out when the time period was over, claimed he was going to wet his pants while sitting in time-out, and shouted, "I hate my mom!" when in time-out. However, the Smiths were equally creative problem solvers. Each time Tim tried a new trick to disrupt time-out, John and Barbara sat down and discussed how to handle it.

Gradually, time-out became a straightforward procedure that the Smiths used for occasional instances of noncompliance and as a way for Tim to calm down when he became upset and disruptive. In fact, Tim sometimes would even put himself in time-out in order to calm down when he became upset with his sister. He was beginning to find ways to control his own behavior to keep himself out of trouble.

The Jones Family

When we last visited the Jones family, Patricia had realized there were many directions she did not need to give to Lisa. Patricia also noticed that when she did give directions, Lisa would comply if they were simple, logical, and straightforward. For Patricia, time-out was not a new concept. However, she learned that she had not been using time-out appropriately. Patricia had always felt it was important to lecture Lisa before and after time-out in order to make sure Lisa understood what was wrong about her behavior. She later explained, "It seemed logical to me to spend time with Lisa going over and over what was wrong with her behavior. That's why I never thought time-out worked. Time-out with lots of lectures appeared to only increase her bad behavior. I never realized I was giving her attention when the whole purpose of time-out was to keep her from receiving attention."

Patricia sat down with Lisa and clearly outlined the time-out procedure, when it would be imposed, and exactly for what behaviors it would be imposed. After that, she rarely had to use time-out. Lisa no longer needed to push her mother in order to see what she could get away with.

Practicing Your Time-Out Skills

Worksheet 9-1 summarizes your daily assignments for using time-out with your child's noncompliance during week 5. It also provides for practice in using time-out to manage other behaviors in the home and in public places.

Assignments for Week 5 and Beyond: Time-Out		**WORKSHEET 9-1**							
		Days of Week 5						*Weeks*	
Tasks	1	2	3	4	5	6	7	7	9
1. Select time-out place	☐								
2. Memorize the steps of time-out	☐								
3. Practice time-out without your child	☐	☐	☐						
4. Tell your child about time-out for noncompliance			☐						
5. Begin using time-out for failure to comply with one direction				☐	☐	☐	☐		
6. Begin using time-out for failure to comply with all directions							☐		
7. Begin using time-out for other problem behaviors in the home								☐	
8. Begin using time-out for problem behaviors in public places									☐

As you carry out these assignments, remember to continue at least one ten-minute daily practice session in attending, rewarding, and ignoring.

Start on day 1 by selecting a time-out place and memorizing the time-out procedure. On the first three days of this week, learn the time-out procedure by studying and practicing. Plan to allow at least thirty minutes a day. Reread this chapter, in particular Tables 9-2 and 9-3. Practice the time-out procedure with your spouse or some other adult by completing the following tasks:

- Describe where and why you selected a particular location for time-out.
- Describe the time-out procedure step by step as it is presented in Table 9-2 and described earlier in this chapter.
- Describe how you will handle problems that arise in time-out as presented in Table 9-3.
- Walk the adult through the entire time-out procedure as presented in Table 9-2. Note any mistakes you make, and go through the entire procedure again.
- Walk the adult through the entire time-out procedure but have her display problem behaviors going to and in time-out. Note any mistakes you make handling these problems, and rehearse again.

On day 3, go over the time-out procedures, as described in Table 9-2, with your child. Walk him through the entire time-out procedure so he will know exactly what to expect. Tell him there are two important rules he must follow when in time-out: (1) stay in the time-out chair without his feet touching the floor and (2) remain quiet.

Select a direction that you often issue to your child and that he often fails to follow. Tell him that time-out will occur every time he does not follow this direction. Then, using the time-out procedure outlined in Table 9-2, give your child a time-out whenever he does not follow the direction. After using time-out with this behavior on days 3 through 6, tell your child that all failure to follow directions at home will result in time-out. Begin using time-out with all such noncompliance.

Post two things on the wall where you will see them every day: a copy of the time-out procedure in Table 9-2 and a calendar. Refresh your memory daily by reading the time-out procedure. On the calendar, record each time you use time-out and the behavior for which you used it. This will help you keep track of how often you use time-out and whether your child's strong-willed problem behaviors are changing.

After two weeks of using time-out in response to noncompliance, begin using it with other problem behaviors you cannot ignore in the home. Set up and explain House Rules for these behaviors. Post your House Rules, in picture form for children who cannot read, on the wall or refrigerator. After about two more weeks of using time-out for problem behaviors in the home, begin using it outside the home.

Learning the details of the time-out procedure will take your full attention. In fact, you will have to be a little strong-willed yourself in order to use it effectively. But if you are attentive to your child and reinforce compliance, you should not have to use time-out very often. Be careful not to revert to focusing only on your child's problem behaviors. Attending and rewarding (especially with praise) will build the positive relationship you want to have with your child.

10

Integrating Your Parenting Skills

Effectively parenting a strong-willed child requires continual effort. Therefore, to help you review the assessment process and the five parenting skills taught in Part II, we have summarized them in Table 10-1. You can use each of these skills as tools to improve your strong-willed child's behavior.

Combining Your New Skills

The skills in the Five-Week Program for Addressing Strong-Willed Behavior should be integrated with one another. Together, these skills provide three basic ways to change strong-willed behavior:

1. You can increase cooperative behavior, which is often incompatible with strong-willed behavior problems, by attending and rewarding.
2. You can decrease strong-willed behavior problems by removing positive consequences for problem behavior through the use of ignoring and time-out.
3. You can reduce noncompliance (a frequent aspect of strong-willed behavior) by modifying what you do before the behavior—that is, how you issue directions to your child.

The Assessment Process and Five Parenting Skills	TABLE 10-1
Assessment Process	• Does my child's behavior need to change? • Does he often display problem behaviors common among strong-willed children? • Is his behavior a problem in daily situations? • Does he score poorly on the Compliance Test? • Am I often frustrated with his behavior?
Skill 1: Attending	• Describe your child's appropriate behavior. • Imitate your child's play behavior. • Reduce directions and questions. • Practice!
Skill 2: Rewarding	• Continue to describe and imitate your child's appropriate behavior. • Verbally reward your child's appropriate behavior by praising him and labeling the desired behavior. • Practice!

It is through the *combined* use of these three procedures that you will most effectively improve your child's strong-willed behavior. With any behavior problem, you need to assess what you are doing before the behavior and what you can do more effectively after the behavior. After the behavior, most of your solutions should combine skills (attends and rewards) to increase desirable behavior, with the use of ignoring or time-out to decrease negative strong-willed behavior.

Let's look at an example. Suppose you are having difficulty with your child in the grocery store. He is demanding candy and running away from you when you do not let him have it. To assess how you are handling this situation, ask questions that concern your use of each of the

	TABLE 10-1 continued
Skill 3: Ignoring	• Decide which behaviors you can ignore. • No physical contact. • No verbal contact. • No eye contact. • Practice!
Skill 4: Giving Directions	• Get your child's attention and make eye contact. • Use a firm, but not loud or gruff, voice. • Give a direction that is specific and simple. • Use physical gestures when appropriate. • Reward compliance. • Practice!
Skill 5: Time-Out	• Choose a time-out location. • Memorize the steps of time-out. • Practice without your child. • Tell your child about time-out for noncompliance and other problem behaviors. • Begin using time-out in the home. • Begin using time-out outside the home.

ways for changing negative strong-willed behavior: Am I attending to and rewarding my child's cooperative behavior? When he does demand candy, am I giving in to his requests or telling him "no" and then ignoring his behavior? If he runs away from me, have I told him such behavior will result in a time-out *and* am I actually using time-out for such behavior? When we enter the store, am I giving him clear directions concerning the behavior I expect from him? By answering these questions, you identify what you are doing and what you should be doing. In this way, you are considering all five of the skills taught in the program and how to combine them to address a particular strong-willed behavior of your child.

In our clinical work, we talk to parents about the importance of consistency in using the skills taught in the Five-Week Program for Addressing Strong-Willed Behavior. If you *consistently* acknowledged your child's positive behaviors through attends and rewards, ignored minor inappropriate behaviors, issued clear directions, and used time-out for inappropriate behaviors that cannot be ignored, you would be the perfect parent! Under these conditions and within the context of your child's temperament and your broader family environment, you would achieve the maximum possible change in your child's negative strong-willed behavior. However, we have never met or heard about the perfectly consistent parent, and you are not likely to be the first one. Instead, work to be as consistent as possible, but realize that you will not be perfect.

The Smith and Jones Families

After their parents participated in the parenting program, were Tim Smith and Lisa Jones "perfect" children? Of course not. Especially in Tim's case, the Smiths had to continually regroup and return to the basics of the program to solve new problems. This required them to discuss each new problem, develop a plan using the skills they learned in the program for handling the problem, and work together to implement the plan. This strategy did not eliminate each new problem behavior, but they were able to diminish the problems. Barbara and John knew Tim would never be as easy as his sister, Susan; however, they began to feel competent as parents and ready for the birth of their third child.

Although Lisa was not perfect either, Patricia did not have to solve problems nearly as often as the Smiths did. When Patricia had finished the five-week program, Lisa's behavior continued to improve, with few setbacks. But like the Smiths, Patricia became a long-term problem solver and began to feel competent as a parent.

The Five Skills in Context

As the Smith and Jones families learned, the parenting skills of the Five-Week Program for Addressing Strong-Willed Behavior do not get perfect results. That is partly because no parent is perfect. Also, parents must exercise those skills within a larger context. As summarized in Table 10-2, the child's behavior is influenced not only by parents' responses but also by the child's temperament and the overall home environment.

You will be most effective as a parent if you use the skills from the five-week program within a positive home environment (the topic of Part III). If you instead argue frequently with your spouse or ex-spouse in front of your child, your use of the parenting skills will be less effective. Or if you use the parenting skills but fail to develop patience or effective communication with others, your child's strong-willed behavior will be more resistant to change. Parenting skills such as those taught in the Five Week Program for Addressing Strong-Willed Behavior are necessary for changing your child's negative strong-willed behavior, but these skills alone are not sufficient. Rather, the total family environment of your home is important.

Your child's temperament (the topic of Part I) also cannot be ignored. You can consider his temperament as an indicator of how much effort will be required to change his strong-willed behavior. The more difficult your child's temperament in such areas as persistence, reactivity, adaptability, and emotionality, the harder you will have to work to change his negative strong-willed behavior. Furthermore, his temperament also may determine how much change in his negative strong-willed behavior you will achieve. A very difficult temperament probably lim-

TABLE 10-2

The Context of Strong-Willed Behavior

Dimension	Broad Role	Specific Means of Fulfilling Role
Temperament	Sets stage for strong-willed behavior	• Defines amount of effort that will be required to change negative strong-willed behavior • Helps define expectations for changes in your child's strong-willed behavior
Parenting Skills	Address strong-willed behavior problems	• Attention to positive behaviors • Rewards for positive behaviors • Ignoring of minor inappropriate behaviors • Appropriate directions • Time-out for inappropriate behavior
Positive Family Environment	Facilitates change of strong-willed behavior	• Adaptive handling of family stressors • Fun with your child • Routines, traditions, and rituals • Good communication skills inside and outside of the home • Patience • Focus on building your child's self-esteem

its how much change will occur in his behavior. In essence, your child's temperament should be an important indicator of your expectations for his behavior. For that reason, Barbara and John Smith had different short- and long-term expectations for Tim (a child with a difficult temperament) than Patricia Jones had for Lisa (whose temperament was less difficult).

To review the dimensions of strong-willed behavior, temperament can be viewed as laying the groundwork. That is, it can set the stage for strong-willed behavior to develop, it informs you of how hard you will have to work to change behavior, and it indicates what expectations are reasonable for changing your child's strong-willed behavior. Within this context, you can apply the skills you learned from the Five-Week Program for Addressing Strong-Willed Behavior. These skills, when used in combination, can lead to changes in your child's strong-willed behavior within the limits defined by his temperament. Finally, a negative family environment will hinder improvement in your child's strong-willed behavior. A positive family environment, in contrast, will make such change easier. Making your home environment more positive is the focus of Part III.

Therefore, your new parenting skills should help you prepare to address problem behaviors of your strong-willed child. However, using the parenting skills and maintaining a positive home environment do not guarantee that your child will be "problem free." Children will be children and, in particular, strong-willed children will be strong-willed! More realistically, your parenting skills and a positive home environment should reduce the number of behavior problems you have to address. Furthermore, when the problems do arise, you will have the skills to assess and address them. You also will have more opportunity to help your child take advantage of the positive aspects of being strong-willed. These results are most likely when you use the parenting skills consistently over time.

PART III

Creating a
Positive Climate
for Behavior Change

The five-week program described in Part II for improving
your child's strong-willed behavior will be most effective
only when you use it together with other positive
parenting approaches. Since many factors influence
children's behavior, behavior management techniques
alone are not enough to drastically change the negative
aspects of a child's strong-willed behavior. The parenting
techniques presented in Part II will be much more
effective when you also enhance the positive atmosphere
in your home. Part III provides our views on how you
can make your home more positive (Chapter 11),
communicate more effectively (Chapter 12), develop
greater patience in dealing with your child (Chapter 13),
and encourage your child's positive self-esteem
(Chapter 14).

11

Creating a More Positive Home

The more positive your home and the more positively your child views you, the more effectively you will guide your child's behavior and personal development. This chapter focuses on positive parenting strategies that increase your strong-willed child's chance for success. We start by looking at parenting from a historical perspective.

What Can We Learn from Past Generations?

Before the Industrial Revolution, family life in America was very different and in many ways more positive than it is today. Although life could be hard, in earlier times family life was often structured by necessity and involved a great deal of interaction between parents and children. Most young families lived in rural areas near grandparents and other extended-family members. Family members typically provided strong support for each other, with many working together on the farm or in some type of family enterprise. Young children spent many hours during the day interacting with their parents and members of the extended family.

Children usually had clearly defined and well-established roles within the family. They were expected to work and make significant contributions to the family at a very young age. Young children helped with cleaning, cooking, and general housekeeping activities. As they became older, children helped in the fields or in some type of activity outside the home. In fact, the two- to three-month summer vacation that children have from school today was started so that they could help their parents on the farm during growing season. These work activities often involved a great deal of interaction with their parents. Working side-by-side with their parents, children learned not only job skills they would need as they grew up, but also a sense of responsibility. Having a meaningful role within the family helped children develop a sense of belonging, self-confidence, and self-discipline.

After working all day together, families typically spent the evenings interacting in other ways. They often used this time for making crafts, telling stories, and relaxing as a family. In other words, family-centered activities were often the focus of nonworking time. The family honored its rituals and traditions, passing them down from generation to generation. Older extended-family members spent much time telling stories about the family, which helped impart a sense of belonging and family loyalty.

In most cases communities were very close and community members supported each other, making the community into a large extended family. In such communities, children typically developed a strong sense of security and belonging, which are the early foundations necessary for the development of positive self-esteem. The importance of community support in rearing children has long been recognized and can be heard in the African proverb "It takes a whole village to raise a child."

In summary, parents and children in the past spent great amounts of time interacting, children had important roles within the family, and families were closely connected to themselves, their past, and their community.

Through these positive interactions and life experiences, children learned the life skills and developed the integrity necessary for their future.

Positive Homes in Today's Society

Our society has witnessed incredible change over the last fifty years, much of it good. However, many of the changes have had a negative impact on families and children. Changes such as long working hours outside the home, moves away from the extended family, family isolation within communities, increased divorce rates, substance abuse, and the prominent role of television in our lives have made it more difficult for parents and children to interact in a way that prepares children for the new world they will be facing. Such changes in our society make it more difficult for children to learn from parent-child interactions and from the assumption of meaningful roles within the family, which lead to such positive attributes as respect, responsibility, self-discipline, values, good judgment, perseverance, and self-confidence. As a result, you must plan and work very hard to provide your strong-willed child with the types of interactions and life experiences that will help instill many of the positive attributes once taught as a matter of course.

It is critical that your strong-willed child view his family and home as safe, secure, loving, and enjoyable. To help your child develop positive character and learn important life skills, you must interact with him frequently and positively. Unfortunately, with all the pressures of today's society, parents often have great difficulty finding time to spend with their children. Even when we find time, we often have difficulty putting aside our own concerns and worries so that our time with our children can be really positive. A lot of us tend to bring work home with us. Even if we don't bring home actual work that needs to be completed, we may be so preoccupied with problems at work or other issues in our lives that we can't really relax and fully enjoy being with our family. When this occurs, it harms your child. If this is a problem for you, you will need to develop strategies for managing the stressful issues in your life so that you can spend more time interacting with your children positively.

Although no home can be stress-free, you must make sure that your stress does not "pollute" your home. This pollution can take many forms, including frequent conflict, impatience, anger, withdrawal, moodiness, excessive alcohol use, or drug abuse. Children need a positive and enjoyable home. Your child needs to view you as being in control and being able to handle life's problems. When you can manage the frustrations in your work and home life effectively, you are teaching you child valuable life skills by example. Your child will soon face increasing concerns and worries, and he will have learned from you how to handle stressful situations—whether or not your own skills are good ones.

Unlike parents of past generations, who had a lot of time and opportunities to teach their children by example, you must learn to teach the same life skills and to build the same character in your child with less time and fewer natural opportunities. It is especially important that you make the time and develop the opportunities because, unfortunately, the society in which your child is growing up is fraught with violence and uncertainty. In a typical day in the United States, approximately 10 children die from guns, 30 are wounded by guns, 135,000 bring a weapon to school, 1,500 drop out of school, 1,800 are abused or neglected, 3,300 run away from home, and 7,700 teenagers become sexually active. Given such a distressing situation, it is easy to see why you must teach your child skills for living in a society that can be violent and frightening.

What is the best way to interact with your child to teach him important life skills and develop strong character? Like everyone else, strong-willed children hate being lectured to. So just telling him what he needs to know or do will not be effective. The most effective way to teach your strong-willed child is by developing a strong relationship with him and *then* helping him learn through experience and example. The first step in this learning process cannot be overemphasized: develop a strong and positive relationship with your child if you want to have his respect. Unfortunately, children are not born with respect for their parents; it is something that has to be earned. If you have your child's respect and he values your relationship, he will want to learn from your example.

Having Fun with Your Child

You can strengthen your relationship with your strong-willed child by having fun with him. It is important to find activities that you both enjoy. Remember, *you* must enjoy the activities, too! If you don't, the activities will become a chore rather than a means for further developing the positive relationship between you and your child.

These activities should be interactive. In other words, the activities should be things you and your child do together. Some examples of interactive activities are presented in Table 11-1.

The purpose of these activities is not just to have fun with your child. Having fun is critical, but the goal is to strengthen the relationship. This will occur if you think of FUN as having three goals: Friendship, Understanding, and Nurturing.

In this context, *friendship* means that you both enjoy being with each other and want to spend time together. It also means conveying a sense of interest and caring. Through friendships we learn more about how to compromise and share, and we develop a sense of acceptance and well-being. Friends also feel more comfortable in disclosing and asking important questions of each other.

Examples of Interactive Activities	**TABLE 11-1**
Rock collecting	Exploring the woods
Woodworking	Cooking
Sports card collecting	Going to a special park
Crafts	Gardening and growing
Jigsaw puzzles	vegetables
Going to sports events	Participating in sports
Bike/trike riding	Hiking
Board games	Building models
Team singing or reading	Scavenger hunts
Fishing	Camping
Picnics	Going to the library
Playing word games	Learning magic tricks
Art projects	Exercising
Kite making and flying	Building snowmen
Sledding	Skating
Making toys	Playing make-believe
Learning sign language	Coin collecting
Stamp collecting	Keeping a family diary
Puppet shows	Making books (artwork,
Listening to story tapes	stories)
Sandbox play	Reading books together

Being a friend to your child leads to you becoming an "askable parent." An askable parent does not withdraw love or support if what she is hearing is disappointing or less than "appropriate" behavior. A child feels comfortable asking this parent any type of question without fear of ridicule or rejection. Askable parents help their child solve problems by examining alternatives *with* him. Such a relationship is necessary if we want our child to learn from us instead of others. Also, developing a strong friendship with your child does not mean you lose your authority. Instead, you are in a position to guide your child toward sound decisions.

The second goal of having fun with your child is to develop greater *understanding* of each other. Through interactive and fun activities, you both learn how to cooperate, understand each other's strengths and similarities, and develop respect for each other. You can use the fun activities to gain a greater appreciation of your child's strengths. Then, you should let your child know that you have become aware of his strengths, and you should try to build upon these strengths. We will discuss this further in Chapter 14.

The third goal of having fun with your child is to *nurture* his development. This includes providing a lot of encouragement and affection. You also help your child develop effective communication skills, social skills, responsibility, values, good judgment, perseverance, self-discipline, and self-confidence. But remember, to be effective in teaching these skills, you must teach through experiences and example, not through lectures. This is one of the most challenging aspects of being an effective parent; it requires a lot of time and ingenuity.

Having FUN is appealing to your child. As a result, you become a stronger role model for him. This is a tremendous responsibility. Your importance as a role model is especially critical during your strong-willed child's early years. As he approaches later childhood and adolescence, your example will be challenged by his peer group and others. You can only hope that the respect you've earned and the example you've provided will have been strong enough to compete with other role models. The importance of trying to impart a sense of morals, responsibility, generosity, empathy, and tolerance during your child's preschool and early school years cannot be overstressed.

The following verse, which is at the entrance to the Louisiana Children's Museum in New Orleans, expresses the importance of teaching your child through play:

> *I tried to teach*
>   *my child with books.*
> *He gave me only*
>   *puzzled looks.*
> *I tried to teach*
>   *my child with words.*

They passed him by
    often unheard.
Despairingly
    I turned aside.
"How shall I teach
    this child?" I cried.
Into my hand
    he put the key.
"Come," he said,
    "play with me."

                    —author unknown

Making the Most Out of Household Jobs

Take advantage of various daily activities that offer a chance to interact with and teach your child. Although fun activities are important, a lot of work needs to be done around the home. Let your child help you with these chores as much as possible. Even very young children can help sweep the floor, push the vacuum cleaner, or set the dinner table. Although doing these jobs yourself is often quicker and more practical, they offer a fantastic teaching opportunity. Doing this work (even if you have to redo the job later) gives your child a sense of contributing to the family and will help him become more responsible and self-confident.

To maintain your strong-willed child's interest in household jobs, you need to offer frequent encouragement and praise. If he is helping you with a task that requires several steps, explain exactly what you are doing. For example, when a lightbulb needs changing, first tell your child you need his assistance. This will build his sense of worth within the family. As you go through the steps, talk about them. This can teach your child not only how to do a specific task but also how to solve problems. You might say, "Let's take the old lightbulb out of the lamp. You take it out by turning it like this. Do you want to help turn it? Next we need to check to see what type of bulb it is. See, right here it says forty watts. Let's go to the kitchen and get a new bulb. See this box, it says forty watts. That's what we need. You carry the new bulb for me. Let me put it in, and then you can turn it until it is tight and will work. Here, you make it tight by turning it like this."

Although this approach takes a lot more time, it is worthwhile. In many ways it is similar to how past generations taught children to feel a sense of worth within their family. If we always do household jobs ourselves while our children watch television or play video games, how can we expect them to develop a sense of responsibility and a sense that their contribution to the family is important?

Communicating "I Love You"

Most of us don't spend enough time communicating our love to our children (or our spouses). While saying "I love you" is important, there are many other effective ways to communicate your love. Here are just a few ideas:

- Leave little signs with hearts or "I ♥ U" on them around the house in places your child will find them (for example, by his bed, on the bathroom mirror, in his coat pocket, in his lunch box).
- Give your child a lot of physical affection. Hugs can really make children feel loved.
- Let your child overhear you talking to someone else about your love for him. This can be more powerful than telling your child directly.
- Start and maintain a family photo or scrap album for your child. This lets him know you think he is important and loved. Put selected photographs, artwork, and other information about your child in the album, and let him keep it in his room.

- Give your child a framed photograph of the family to put in his room.
- Display your child's artwork. Don't let him find those valuable masterpieces in the trash.
- Remember that actions speak louder than words.

Be creative! Spend some time generating a list of ways that will be especially meaningful to *your* child. Every child is different, and developing a personal list of "I love you's" will help you become more sensitive and responsive to his individuality.

Structure and Routines

A positive home has structure and routines. While too much structure and very rigid routines can be stifling, moderate use of structure and routines can contribute to effective family functioning. Children, especially strong-willed children, need structure. Family rules should be clear and specific (for example, walk, do not run, in the house). Parents should be careful not to have an extremely long list of house rules for young children but just a short list of the most important rules.

Children are also creatures of habit. A consistent daily routine will help your strong-willed child establish more appropriate behavior. Your child should go to bed at about the same time each night and get up at about the same time every morning. His bedtime routine should be consistent from night to night. The bedtime routine should involve several quieting activities—such as bath, story, prayer—that occur every night in the same sequence. Morning dressing routines and mealtimes should be as consistent as possible. Establishing clear and consistent structure and routines in your home can help decrease the amount of time you spend nagging and directing your child.

Family Traditions and Rituals

Homes feel special and more positive when the family has traditions and rituals. However, many families have not kept up their family traditions and rituals from past generations. This is unfortunate, since children often love them, and they can give children a strong sense of family and their roots. Traditions and rituals help define the uniqueness of a family and help children view their family as special. Examples of traditions might include a special way for the family to celebrate holidays, such as having a family picnic every July 4, having a family Halloween party every year, or family caroling every Christmas Eve. Also fun are unique traditions that you create for your family. For example, you might have small celebrations for children's half birthdays; when a child turns five and a half, he receives special privileges that day.

We also strongly recommend celebrating a holiday from the country of your family's origin. This can be combined with learning more about the country (or countries) of your family's origin, an enjoyable activity while at the same time teaching family members about their family's heritage. Holiday traditions also can be made special by having certain food, decorations, and activities. Children will often long remember such things as having the holiday meal by candlelight, kissing under the mistletoe, or playing a special game, particularly when such activities occur only on that holiday.

Also plan for more frequent family rituals. During each night's dinner you could have each person take a turn telling the family about something he or she did that day. You could have a certain time of week (for instance, Sunday afternoon) when the family does something together. These simple traditions and rituals can become a rich time for positive family interactions.

If you want to develop some traditions and rituals for your family, remember to keep them positive and of interest to children and adults alike. What you want to do is to create activities that your children will look back upon and cherish when they are adults. Hopefully, they will be something your children will do with your grandchildren so that your family traditions and rituals will be passed on to future generations.

The Mother-Father Relationship

The relationship between a mother and father has a profound impact on children. As discussed in Chapter 3, research has shown that problems such as frequent and/or intense parental conflict harm children. Therefore, parents should nurture their relationship with each other.

To do this, you must be a friend not only to your child but also to your spouse. Being friends with your spouse means having someone who supports you and someone you can open up to, count on, have fun with, and share life with. Unfortunately, over time the pressures of life often interfere with this friendship, and it takes a backseat to other demands.

As in your relationship with your child, one of the most effective ways to rekindle or enhance the relationship with your spouse is to increase your fun together. Having fun together is a critical component of the courting period, but after marriage and children many couples spend less and less time having fun together. Having fun is very important. In fact, the amount of fun couples have together has been found to be the strongest factor in overall marital happiness.

How do you have more fun together? The primary way is that the two of you *must* make time for fun activities. Plan dates with your spouse, but don't use these dates as a time to discuss or resolve problems. Try to relax and have fun together. It may help to make lists of fun things you want to do together, so that when the time comes for you to be alone, you'll have a number of activities from which to choose. The list should include activities that are enjoyable for *both* of you. Therefore, you must prepare the list together, and both of you must be honest about what is fun. We recommend that the two of you really brainstorm. Come up with some practical fun activities (for example, going out for dinner, taking a moonlight stroll, looking at old photo albums) *and* some exotic fun activities (renting a cabin in the mountains, going to a tropical island). You never know, you might actually try an exotic activity once you begin thinking about it!

If the two of you have fun together, it will be obvious to your child. This is very important. He will identify family life as a happy and fun time, and his images of marital relationships will be positive.

Beyond having fun together, you and your spouse should try to develop ways of dealing with conflict so it does not become intense or occur frequently in your child's presence. This might involve agreeing ahead of time to walk away from each other when disagreements start to escalate in front of your child. You might want to agree on a secret signal that you both can use to indicate that a disagreement is escalating into intense conflict. When you use the signal, you and your spouse should pull back and discuss the issue later when your child is not present. An example of such a signal would be a tug on the ear (your own ear, not your partner's!). Although frequent and/or intense parental conflict is harmful to children, they actually can benefit from occasionally observing their parents disagree on an issue. A little disagreement is valuable if parents go on to resolve their differences or agree to disagree without launching into a fight or putting each other down. By observing his parents, the child can learn conflict resolution skills.

For parents who are divorced, it is just as critical (if not more so) to avoid conflict in their child's presence. This might mean developing systems to avoid open conflict, such as communicating information through notes when one parent comes to pick up or drop off the child. Try to identify when the conflict is most likely to occur (say, when picking the child up), and develop a strategy to avoid conflict at those times. Since divorced parents cannot model how to engage in fun activities together, it is even more important for them to reduce conflict in front of their child.

How Important Are Fathers?

Whether it is right or wrong, mothers in our society typically assume the major responsibility for rearing young children. This emphasis on the maternal role in child rearing and the decline of two-parent families resulted in many professionals questioning the importance of the father's role in children's development. Almost all parenting research in the past focused on mothers. Fortunately, this void has been recognized, and researchers are now putting more emphasis on the potential contributions of fathers to children's development.

From this emerging research area, we now know that fathers do have a significant impact on the development of their children. Not surprisingly, their influence can be positive or negative. In some areas, fathers may even have a greater impact on their children than mothers. For instance, in a recent study, one of us (R.F.) found that the level of acceptance a father expressed toward his child significantly predicted how well the child did in school, while the mother's level of acceptance did not have a significant impact. (This doesn't mean that the mother's level of acceptance is unimportant to a child. Rather, each parent's level of acceptance is probably related to different areas of a child's adjustment.)

Because the parenting styles of *both* parents affect children, fathers, whether married or divorced, must be actively involved and strive to be a positive influence in their child's life. Fathers cannot avoid active involvement in parenting their young children by saying that it's the mother's job or that their input does not matter. Fathers *do* make a difference!

Community Networking

It sometimes seems that the closer we live to our neighbors, the less familiar we are with them. Families from past generations tended to be supportive and emotionally close to other families in their rural community, but in modern cities families often know only one or two of their neighbors. This is significant. Research has shown that, as families become more isolated, problems within the family tend to increase. This is likely because families who have close contact with other families tend to be supportive of each other and provide help with problems. This support may come in various forms. Families may share parenting information such as names of sitters, provide emotional support, or simply have fun together.

If you feel somewhat isolated within your community, take the initiative to network and reach out to other young families. Many parents have found that starting a play group for their young children is an excellent means of support. Play groups typically involve four or five families with toddlers or preschoolers. The parents and children get together for a couple of hours every week. This provides a regular opportunity for parents to give and receive support and for the children to play together and develop friendships. Whether you get involved in a play group or some other activity, it is important that you somehow network with other parents in your community.

As a parent, you need support such as this because you play a critical role in laying the foundation for your child's learning appropriate behavior and values and developing such characteristics as responsibility, self-confidence, good judgment, and perseverance. To help your child develop these positive characteristics, you should create a positive climate in your home. Get involved with your child, have fun with him, express your love for him, strengthen relationships within your family, and teach your child through example. As these efforts help you create a positive atmosphere in your home, your discipline strategies for behavior problems will become more effective and easier to implement. Perhaps best of all, you will need to use punishment less frequently.

12

Improving Your Communication Skills

Families that communicate effectively tend to have fewer problems, are more likely to address problems successfully when they do arise, and enjoy being with each other more than do families who do not communicate effectively. Effective communication skills are a vital aspect of successful family functioning. Fortunately, many families demonstrate effective communication patterns. However, even in these families, effective patterns are least likely just when they are needed most—during times of stress. Stress can result from various sources, including financial problems, medical problems, emotional problems, difficulties at work, or parenting a strong-willed child.

The demands placed on a family as a result of having a strong-willed child can be very stressful and can lead to the development and escalation of poor communication patterns within the family. Over time, the patterns of poor communication can seriously erode family functioning. This is a snowballing effect: distress leads to poor communication, poor communication leads to greater distress, greater distress leads to even poorer communication, and the cycle continues to escalate. As this cycle continues, conflict increases and family problems worsen.

Having a strong-willed child affects communication among all family members but may be most detrimental

The Strong-Willed Child and Snowballing Ineffective Communication Between Parents

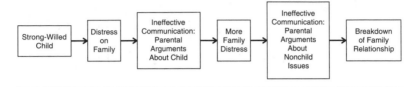

to the communication pattern between parents (whether married or divorced). Parents often end up arguing about discipline at home, problems at child care or preschool, and whom to blame for contributing to their child's behavior. Over time, the problems and distress that arise from having a strong-willed child influence the communication between parents on issues unrelated to their child. In extreme situations, this cycle of poor communication and distress can eventually cause the breakdown of family relationships, as illustrated in the figure at the top of this page. To avoid or at least minimize such family crises, parents must work on improving their communication skills.

Having a strong-willed child also frequently affects parents' communication with others who care for or interact with their child. The stress of trying to meet the needs of a strong-willed child can eventually cause communication breakdowns between a parent and relatives, a parent and child-care workers, and a parent and teachers. Therefore, even in single-parent families where the other parent has minimal or no involvement in child rearing, the parent who is with the child can benefit from trying to improve her communication skills.

Communication Problems and Solutions

In this chapter we will present some common communication problems and recommend solutions to those problems. Changing communication styles can be very difficult, so it will require a major effort. Old habits are hard to break! We recommend identifying only one or two communication problems to work on at a time. Let your partner or a significant other know specifically what skills you are going to work on. Ask this person to help point out to you (very gently!) when you err and to offer positive feedback as you make progress. This process typically works best when the other person is also trying to improve communication, because the two of you can support each other. A supportive atmosphere is *essential* to effectively change communication patterns. An atmosphere of criticism and finger pointing will cause your efforts to fail.

Problem #1: Inattention

Most people would agree that you cannot have a meaningful conversation if one person is not paying attention to what the other person is saying. Although we all recognize the importance of attending to what is being said, inattention is the most common communication problem. Inattention can result from various external and internal factors. External factors include distractions such as interruptions by children, a phone ringing, or a loud television. Internal factors that prevent us from paying attention include fatigue, anger, anxiety, thoughts about something else that is pressing (such as being late for an appointment), or indifference to what the other person has to say.

Inattention to what another person is saying is easy to recognize if you observe the conversation, specifically watching body language. People who are not really listening are often looking away from the person speaking or are making negative facial expressions such as sneers, smirks, glares, or looks of disgust. Inattention is also obvious from the verbal content of conversations. Conversations marked by inattention typically involve frequent interruptions in order to question, argue, or criticize. It is hard to feel that someone is listening to you when she repeatedly interrupts you!

Inattention not only leads to ineffective communication but also to increased frustration and distress. Individuals who do not feel listened to may restate issues over and over, withdraw completely, or lash out in anger.

Solution: Be an Effective Listener

Being a truly good listener is hard. It can require a lot of effort and practice! However, the payoff for becoming a good listener makes it well worth the effort. Most people can accept differing opinions and disagreements as long as they feel their perspective has been heard and understood. Since effective listening is considered to be the most important communication skill, we are going to devote more attention to listening than to some of the other communication skills. To be an effective listener, you should develop a listening style with the following components:

- Eliminate distractions.
- Listen to understand.
- Reflect or summarize what you hear.
- Clarify to reach full understanding.
- Use receptive body language.

When you *eliminate distractions*, you show the person who is talking to you that you are interested in what she is saying. So turn off the television (or at least turn down the volume), put down the newspaper, and eliminate other distractions. If you cannot eliminate distractions immediately, indicate that you really want to hear what the other person has to say. Suggest another time (such as when the children are outside playing) when you will be able to discuss the issue without interruption.

Listen to understand. When people are discussing an issue, they sometimes have their mind already made up about the issue. When this happens, they probably do not really listen to the other person, which can be very frustrating. When this type of communication pattern occurs frequently, it can be devastating to a relationship. Instead, make the effort to *really* listen to understand what the other person is saying. Simply stated, listen for content. Try to separate *what* is being said from *how* it is said. Try to understand the issue from the other person's perspective. Of course, you have the right to disagree, but express your views only after the other person has expressed hers. Remember, the other person is much more likely to respect your disagreement if she feels that you have really listened to, and tried to understand, her perspective.

How can you let the other person know that you have really listened to and tried to understand what she is saying? A useful way to do this is through *reflection and summarization*. Reflection refers to making comments during the course of a conversation that indicate you are really paying attention to what is being said. The father in the following conversation uses reflection:

> Mother: *I feel like I'm at the end of my rope. Jonathan's behavior is driving me crazy. He is constantly trying to get my attention, and he will not stop whining. It's "Mommy do this" and "Mommy do that" all day long. I feel like I spend all day waiting on him.*
> Father: *It must be so frustrating having to deal with him all day long without a break.*
> Mother: *I have never felt so frustrated in my whole life.*

The father simply reflects and labels the emotion the mother just expressed to him. His response communicates that he is listening and trying to understand her perspective.

Summarizing involves stating *in a nonjudgmental way* the overall point the other person was making. It is particularly useful when discussing complex issues or after a lengthy discussion. Let's look at an example:

> *Father: Jonathan's preschool teacher called me at work today to say that Jonathan has been getting into a lot of trouble at school. She said the problems start as soon as he arrives and starts playing with Matthew. When Matthew doesn't do what he wants him to, Jonathan starts calling him names and even pushes and hits him. At snack time he often tries to take Matthew's snack away from him. At recess he pushes Matthew around on the playground. She said that it's really kind of strange that, although Jonathan does all of these things to Matthew, Matthew still likes to be around Jonathan and considers him a friend. What really worries me is that she said the preschool cannot tolerate aggressive behavior. I think she was implying that if Jonathan's behavior doesn't improve, they will kick him out! I don't know what we would do if they ever did kick him out.*
>
> *Mother: Well, it seems as if the major problem is between Jonathan and Matthew, since the teacher didn't say anything about problems with other children. We need to think about what things we can do to address the problem.*

Jonathan's mother did a nice job of summarizing a lengthy, and probably emotional, dialogue by her husband about a complicated issue. Her statement assured her husband that she was listening. Furthermore, she was able to propose an initial plan of action for the problem.

When you *clarify*, or ask pertinent questions about what another person is saying, you increase your understanding of her perspective and also indicate that you are listening. In the example of the parents discussing Jonathan and Matthew in preschool, the mother did not clarify. She assumed that Jonathan was not having any problems with children other than Matthew. To clarify, the mother could have asked if the teacher had mentioned problems with any other children. By asking questions for clarification, you express your interest in trying to fully understand what the other person is saying. Although most of us ask questions for clarification in our jobs and other activities, we are much less likely to do so in our personal relationships, especially when conversations involve stressful family issues. However, the discussion of stressful family issues is perhaps the most important time to ask clarifying questions.

Your *body language* can tell a great deal about how interested you are in what another person is saying. You clearly communicate your lack of interest in what is being said when you do not look at the person who is talking. When you look away, continue to read the newspaper, or watch television when someone is talking to you, you send a strong message: what the person is saying is not important. You also express lack of interest when you mimic or make faces at the person talking. When you express disinterest and disrespect in such ways, the conversation more than likely turns to conflict or just ends. Some ways of expressing interest through body language include maintaining eye contact, facing the person talking, projecting a facial express of interest, nodding occasionally to demonstrate that you agree with certain things that are being said, and avoiding negative facial expressions (or other negative gestures). The nonverbal message is "I respect you enough to listen and try to understand your perspective."

Problem #2: Monopolizing the Conversation

It is hard to carry on a real conversation when one person monopolizes the conversation. We have all tried to have conversations where the other person would not let us get a word in edgewise. A dominant talker may be fine in certain social conversations, but this behavior presents a problem when two people are discussing an issue of importance to both of them. If you monopolize conversations and are only interested in gaining support for your own views and opinions, the other person will probably begin to feel resentful, and her frustration will build. At this point, she is likely to become angry, and communication probably will break down.

Solution: Request Feedback and Take Turns Talking

Individuals who monopolize conversations tend to be more extroverted and talkative. If you are a "talker" and monopolize conversations, you may need to take steps to involve others more. This is especially true when you are talking to someone who tends to be quiet and introverted and who may be reluctant to interrupt you to express her views and opinions.

When you are discussing an issue with someone, make an effort to solicit her opinions and views. In doing so, avoid questions that encourage simple "yes" or "no" answers. For example, saying, "You agree with me, don't you?" encourages the other person to simply say yes. These types of questions are called closed-ended questions. Instead, try to ask questions that promote dialogue. Questions that promote conversations begin with the words *how, when, what,* or *why.* Such questions are commonly referred to as open-ended questions. Some examples of closed-ended and open-ended questions are in Table 12-1. Open-ended questions encourage the other person to express her views or opinions. Also make sure that you allow the other person her full turn in expressing her views and opinions without interrupting her (no matter how much you might want to!).

Problem #3: Silence

On the opposite extreme from people who monopolize conversations are those who remain silent. Many of these people try to avoid conflict or disapproval by remaining silent. Not speaking does avoid conflict and disapproval in the short run. However, if you let feelings

Closed- Versus Open-Ended Questions	TABLE 12-1

Closed-Ended Questions	Open-Ended Questions
"Did you have a good day at work/school?"	"*What* did you do at work/school today?"
"Do you think his behavior is getting worse?"	"*Why* do you think his behavior seems to be getting worse?"
"Did he stop the tantrum?"	"*How* did you get him to stop the tantrum?"
"Do you think I should talk to him about . . . ?"	"*When* do you think would be the best time to talk to him about . . . ?"

bottle up inside you, you are likely to reach a point where you explode in anger. This certainly does not improve communication!

Solution: Speak Up

You can avoid angry outbursts from bottled-up feelings by expressing your feelings and opinions as they arise during conversations. This is difficult for many people. If you are someone for whom speaking up does not come naturally, you will have to plan how to speak up before you actually can do it. Here is a plan for learning how to speak up in conversations:

- Think about the worst thing that can happen if you speak your opinion. It rarely is horrible.
- Think about the good things that can happen if you express your opinion. These include effective communication and prevention of bottled-up feelings.
- Plan to express your opinion in a conversation with one particular person, ideally someone who is likely to be supportive.
- Do it and evaluate the consequences. They will not be as bad as you think.

If you continue this pattern, eventually you will not have to plan to express yourself.

Problem #4: Being Judgmental

Many of us have very strong opinions about numerous issues. If you are one of these people, others may be reluctant to express differing views. They may believe you are not open to considering other views and will judge them negatively. In such situations the other person often withdraws from the conversation. This person will probably build up resentment toward you over time. This does not help the relationship or the development of effective communication between the two of you.

Solution: Express Openness to Listen to Other Views

Although you may have strong opinions regarding certain issues, demonstrate a willingness to hear other opinions. This does not mean that you are going to change your opinions, just that you are willing to listen to opposing viewpoints. Avoid putting down the other person when he expresses a differing opinion. Discuss the concerns you have about his idea, rather than attacking him as a person. When listening to other perspectives, try to keep an open mind as much as possible. At some later point, on some issue, the other person may convince you that he is right! None of us is ever too old to learn.

Problem #5: Dwelling on Past Problems During Conflicts

When we are discussing a conflict, some of us tend to bring up past conflicts. For example, you might catch yourself saying, "It's just like when you. . . ." When you repeatedly air someone's "dirty laundry," it makes her feel as if she will never be forgiven for past transgressions.

This can lead to a lot of negative feelings and to a break-down in communication.

Solution: Stick to the Present Issue

When discussing problems, try to focus on the problem at hand. Avoid bringing up past problems that are not directly and importantly related to the present. For a relationship to flourish, the people involved must be willing to forgive. We all make mistakes. Hopefully, we can learn from them without having to be repeatedly reminded about them. Try to be forgiving and live in the present, not the past!

Problem #6: Focusing on Who Is to Blame

In our society we often want to focus on who is to blame for a problem. This concern with blame occurs at the national, local, and family levels However, whether the problem is the federal budget deficit or a child's behavior, most major problems result from a number of factors. Trying to identify or focus on who is to blame is rarely productive. Finger pointing usually leads to hurt feelings, not solutions to a problem.

Solution: Focus on Developing Solutions to Problems

Rather than assessing blame for a problem, it is much more effective to focus on potential solutions for the problem. For instance, if four-year-old Richard has been heard using foul language repeatedly, it will be much more productive for the parents to focus on developing a united approach for dealing with the problem, rather than blaming each other for the times they have each used foul language in Richard's presence. In such cases, it is certainly acceptable to discuss factors that may be playing a role, such as overhearing others using foul language, as long as the focus is on identifying solutions and not on finger pointing. Because most problems, including those related to a child's behavior, result from many factors, the answer is rarely simple, and placing blame will not solve the problem.

Problem #7: Cross-Complaining

When someone complains about something you have done, a common reaction is to complain about something that person has done. For example, if you complain about your spouse's lack of help with the housework, your spouse may complain about your lack of affection. The philosophy behind such cross-complaining is that the best defense is a good offense. That is, the way to protect myself when verbally attacked is to counterattack. Unfortunately, instead of solving a problem, cross-complaining often escalates into an argument.

Solution: Work on the Current Issue

It's hard to accept another person's complaint about you or your behavior without getting at least somewhat upset. Still, try to rise above your initial emotional reaction, and resist the temptation to lash back. If you can avoid cross-complaining and focus on the issue at hand, you have a much better chance of successfully addressing the current problem. If you disagree with what the other person is saying, discuss the issue from a problem-solving perspective. Try to understand the complaint from the other person's point of view. Listen to exactly what the person is saying and ask yourself why the person is saying it. Is there any truth in what she is saying? Discuss what each of you can do to avoid the same problem in the future.

Problem #8: Mind Reading

At times many of us assume we just know what another person is thinking. Assumptions are especially likely among people who know each other well. If you start assuming you know what another person is thinking, you are heading down a dangerous path. If you have not asked, you will never know for sure what she is thinking. When you say, "I know what you're thinking," or, "I know you think . . . ," it puts the other person on the defensive. Over time a lot of resentment can develop if you are repeatedly speaking someone's mind.

Solution: Speak Only for Yourself

During conversations, especially those that involve some level of conflict, speak only for yourself. Let others express their own opinions. You also may want to encourage others to express their opinions by asking them what they think. Avoid interrupting them when they begin to speak. Do not assume you know what others are thinking and are about to say!

Problem #9: Disrespect and Put-Downs

Unfortunately, people tend to show less respect for loved ones than for casual acquaintances. Most of us are generally polite and respectful toward people we do not know very well. However, knowing someone well might make you feel as if you have permission to be less than respectful. This disrespect often includes put-downs such as "You're lazy," "You're stupid," or even "You're worthless."

Solution: Be Polite and Use "I" Messages

If you treat the people you love with respect, you will greatly reduce the amount of conflict in your relationships. Make every effort to be as polite to those you love as you are to others. Try to express rather than vent your feelings. When you find yourself about to say something that would be a put-down to another person, rethink the message and say it in a less threatening way. How can you do this?

It is more effective to describe how we feel about a problem than to hurl accusations. Describing how you feel is often referred to as the use of "I" messages—that is, statements about yourself, which begin with the word *I*. These types of messages communicate your feelings or needs. "You" messages, on the other hand, are about the person you are talking to; they begin with the word *you*. Such statements often blame or criticize the other person. Let's look at an example of these two types of messages:

"You" message	"You are such a slob. You just throw your stuff all over the place, and you never help clean up."
"I" message	"I get so frustrated about the house being such a mess. I feel like I constantly need to clean up, but I just don't have the time to do it myself. I really need some help."

Think about how much more willing you would be to help clean up after hearing this "I" message instead of the "you" message! Although "I" messages cannot solve all communication problems, they can minimize conflict and encourage healthier patterns of communication.

Problem #10: Mixed Messages

Imagine your spouse tells you she is interested in what you have to say, but she does not look at you when you are talking. Your spouse's behavior is inconsistent with her words. When verbal and nonverbal messages conflict in this way, what message do you get? Mixed messages can be hard to interpret.

Research suggests that people will give at least as much weight to your nonverbal messages as to your verbal ones. Albert Mehrabian found that only 7 percent of what we communicate is done through words, 38 percent through nonverbal vocal characteristics such as tone and volume, and 55 percent through body movements such as facial expressions. Regardless of the exact percentages, nonverbal communication is very important.

Solution: Use Consistent Verbal and Nonverbal Messages

To be understood correctly, make sure your verbal and nonverbal messages are consistent. For example, if you are saying something positive, your nonverbal language also needs to be positive. Positive nonverbal language includes facial expressions (such as smiling and looking empathic), body language (such as touching or leaning toward the person), and tone of voice (for example, warm, joyful, caring, or happy).

Putting Solutions into Action

As we mentioned at the beginning of this chapter, changing your patterns of communication is often very difficult. To give you a handy reference, Table 12-2 summarizes the ten communication problems and solutions we have discussed. Review them and decide which areas are problems for you. Also get feedback from others. One way to do this is to ask your spouse or a friend to indicate which of the solutions in Table 12-2 are strengths of yours. You then may assume that the other areas are the ones on which you should focus.

After identifying specific problems and potential solutions, you may need to establish a structured approach to learn how to use the solutions. This approach might include practicing with a tape recorder or video camera, role-playing with someone, or using planned discussions. Planned discussions involve selecting a time and place free from distraction where you can discuss specific issues with your spouse or close friend in order to practice

Review of Communication Problems and Solutions

TABLE 12-2

Problem	Solution
Inattention	Be an effective listener.
Monopolizing the conversation	Request feedback and take turns talking.
Silence	Speak up.
Being judgmental	Express openness to listen to other views.
Dwelling on past problems during conflicts	Stick to the present issue.
Focusing on who is to blame	Focus on developing solutions to problems.
Cross-complaining	Work on one problem at a time.
Mind reading	Speak only for yourself.
Disrespect and put-downs	Be polite and use "I" messages.
Mixed messages (inconsistent verbal and nonverbal messages)	Use consistent verbal and nonverbal messages.

the communication skills you are trying to master. For some suggestions to incorporate into your planned discussions, see the box titled "Does Your Communication Style Need Improvement?" Try to apply these tips to *all* of your conversations!

Being an effective communicator is difficult, but if you learn the skills presented in this chapter, you can improve your communication style. These skills will not only improve your ability to communicate but also indirectly may improve the behavior of your strong-willed child. That is because you will communicate more effectively with your child and will be better able to discuss your concerns about him with others.

Does Your Communication Style Need Improvement?

Nobody is perfect, and that axiom applies to communication as well as to the other things we do. But there are some communication styles that can really turn people off. Pay attention to the way you talk to others this week. How often do you hear yourself using some of these negative communication styles?

- Nagging
- Lecturing
- Interrupting
- Criticizing
- Sarcasm
- Threatening

If you use some of these negative practices, work on improving your communication style. Focus on replacing the negatives with some of these communication builders:

- Be clear and specific in what you say.
- Use "I" messages.
- Ask for feedback about what you are saying.
- Focus on positives.
- Ask questions that promote detailed responses:
  "I'd really like to hear about . . ."
  "Can you tell me more?"
  "What do you think about . . ."
  "Can you explain that to me?"

13

Developing More Patience

Parents of strong-willed children often report that their patience is tested constantly. They have to deal not only with the typical stressors of parenthood, but also with a child who can be very demanding. The constant demands would take their toll on almost any parent's patience! Therefore, it is normal to sometimes lose your patience and feel upset, frustrated, or angry.

Unfortunately, being the parent of a strong-willed child places you in a difficult dilemma. Your child's demanding behavior increases the chance that you will lose your patience, but your child needs you to keep your patience *more* than most other children do. Strong-willed children respond best to parents who can handle problems in a matter-of-fact way. When you lose your patience, you lose control of effectively managing your child's behavior. At these times, you lose your objectivity and your ability to make intelligent decisions. In addition, many children withdraw, due to fear, from parents who frequently lose their patience. Fear of a parent clearly hinders the child's development of a respectful and positive relationship with his parent.

Losing your patience, especially if it happens often, can create significant problems in the long run, even if it sometimes appears to have remedied the situation in the short run. The more patient you can be, especially in the face of your child's disruptive behavior, the more effective you will be as a parent. However, as you well know, this is not easy.

In this chapter we will discuss the relationship between how you think about your child's behavior and how patient you are. Understanding this strong relationship will help you learn to become more patient and, thus, be a more effective parent. After discussing this relationship, we will present ways to improve your patience by changing how you think. Unfortunately, even after learning ways to increase your patience, you probably will lose your patience again at some point. Therefore, we also will discuss what you do when you do lose your patience. Finally, because people lose patience more often when they become stressed, we will conclude the chapter with general strategies to minimize the negative effects of stress in your life.

Patience and the Way You Think

When you are with your child, you probably experience a wide range of emotions. Some are good; some are not so good. Most parents think those feelings are caused by their child's behavior. Suppose your child has a temper tantrum in a store, and you become upset. You might conclude that the temper tantrum caused you to become upset. However, his temper tantrum does not *directly* cause you to become upset. What causes you to become upset is the way you view the temper tantrum.

Let's look at some different ways you might view your child's tantrum. If your child begins a temper tantrum in public and you think that he should always behave himself in public, you might view him as "bad" or "mean," which may lead you to become angry and start yelling at him. Or you might start thinking that others view you as a "bad" mother for not being able to "control" your child. In this case, you might question your ability to be a good

The Cause of Parents' Emotional Reactions

Your child's behavior does not directly cause your emotional reaction.

Your emotional reaction depends on how you think about your child's behavior.

parent, start feeling depressed, and do nothing to address his tantrum because you lack the confidence to take action. A third, and more appropriate, view may be that the tantrum resulted from his being overtired and needing a nap. In this case, you would probably not become very upset but rather decide that it is time to go home so that he can take his nap.

As in this example, your child's behavior in and of itself does not make you become upset or lose your patience. You cause yourself to lose your patience by the way you view his behavior. The figure at the top of the page illustrates this important point.

Certain common ways of thinking about a child's behavior often lead parents to lose their patience:

- "My child should never behave in certain ways."
- "I am a bad parent if my child behaves in certain ways."
- "It is terrible and I can't stand it when my child behaves in certain ways."
- "My child behaves in certain ways to make me suffer."
- "My child should always behave well."
- "My child is always trying to get on my nerves."
- "I need to get angry to correct my child's behavior."

Becoming aware of these thoughts will allow you to identify whether you have similar thoughts that put you at risk
for more easily losing your patience with your child. If you
identify with these thoughts, you should pay special attention to the next section.

Changing Your Negative Thoughts

All children are going to misbehave at times or do things
that their parents do not like. Therefore, it is not terrible
or awful when your child misbehaves, unless you convince yourself that it is terrible or awful. This does not
mean that you should be content with or condone your
child's misbehavior. However, you do need to have a realistic perspective regarding your child's behavior, and you
need to avoid negative absolute thinking.

Negative absolute thinking occurs when you start thinking negatively in absolute ways about something and use
terms that include *should*, *must*, or *always*. For example, a
parent might think, "My child should never misbehave."
But all children are going to misbehave. If you think your
child should never misbehave, you are setting yourself up
to lose your patience and become angry when he does.

Many of us think in negative absolute terms. If you are
one of these parents, try to challenge and change those
thoughts. For example, if you tend to think that your child
should never misbehave, try to think along more reasonable lines when he does misbehave. You might say to yourself, "I don't like it when he behaves like this, but I can
handle it." Also, try to be realistic and acknowledge to
yourself that all children misbehave and it is not terrible
when your child misbehaves. You do not have to like it,
but admit that it is going to happen and that it is undesirable—not terrible. Terrible is when your child is stricken
with a life-threatening illness, not when he has a temper
tantrum at the shopping mall!

Let's look at another common way of thinking in negative absolute terms: thinking other people believe you are a bad parent when your child misbehaves. If you have such a thought, try to challenge it. A more realistic thought is that most parents have had similar experiences and probably empathize with you in such a situation. Even if they do not understand, you do not need the approval of strangers to know that you are a good parent who is doing the best you can with a difficult, strong-willed child. Try to replace your negative absolute thinking with these more realistic thoughts. After all, your worth as a parent is not based on your child's behavior in public places!

Some parents who are prone to negative absolute thoughts find it helpful to consciously start reciting more realistic and helpful thoughts to themselves when their child misbehaves. Here are some sample statements:

- "My child will misbehave sometimes even when he knows the rules."
- "When my child misbehaves, all he has done is broken a rule."
- "Getting angry will not help me effectively deal with my child."
- "It is undesirable and irritating when my child misbehaves, but it is not terrible."
- "I can handle this situation more effectively if I stay calm."
- "I am not a bad parent just because my child broke a rule. All children break rules."

This realistic self-talk helps avoid the trap of thinking negatively out of habit.

Another kind of negative thinking involves making negative assumptions about the intentions of your child's behavior. An example is assuming your child is misbehaving to get back at you for something you did. Although this may occasionally be the case, young children rarely misbehave in order to get revenge or to get on your nerves.

However, when you make such an assumption, you are more likely to lose patience.

Try not to assume the worst. In most cases young children misbehave to get something they want or to avoid something they do not want to do. Their motives are typically self-centered and do not include a desire to upset their parents. This may be hard to believe at times, but it is true!

What to Do When You Lose Your Patience

Almost all parents lose their patience at times. Even if you try really hard to change your negative thoughts, you are likely at some time to lose your patience and become angry. If you think in absolute terms that you should never lose your patience, that you should always be patient, and that it is terrible if you lose your patience, you may very well become upset or depressed when you do lose your patience.

Becoming upset or depressed about your impatience will not help you be patient. Instead, when you lose your patience, acknowledge that it is undesirable and unfortunate but also human. Expecting yourself to always be patient is unreasonable. Do not make excuses for losing your patience, but acknowledge and understand that it is going to happen on occasion.

Since you probably will lose your patience with your child in the future, what can you do to minimize the negative effects? We recommend using the four *R*s of damage control:

1. *Recognize* that you have lost your patience.
2. *Remove* yourself or step back from the situation.
3. *Review* the situation.
4. *Respond* to the situation.

The first step is to *recognize* as soon as possible that you have lost your patience. Since we all react somewhat differently, try to identify your personal signals that indicate you are losing or have lost your patience. Examples of such signals might be a hot flash, a clenched jaw, a clenched fist, a pounding heart, swearing, or starting to raise your voice. The key is to identify that you are losing (or have lost) your patience as early as possible so that you can regain self-control more easily.

The second step is to *remove* yourself from the situation as soon as you recognize that you are losing or have lost your patience. If you are at home or in public with another adult who can assume temporary responsibility for your child, walking away for a few moments may be most effective. Of course, no matter how mad you are, you should never leave your young child unattended in a potentially dangerous situation, such as alone in a public place. When you cannot physically leave the situation, try to step back—literally. Take a couple of steps away from your child, look at something other than your child, and try to regain your composure. Take some deep breaths and try to calm yourself as much as possible. Recite to yourself realistic thoughts about your child's behavior, such as the ones suggested earlier. For example, say to yourself, "My child broke a rule. Getting angry and losing control will not help me effectively deal with this situation." This type of positive self-talk can be very effective in managing anger and regaining self-control.

Once you have gained your self-control, pause and briefly *review* the situation to yourself. Think about what happened, how your thoughts led you to lose your patience, and how you can best handle the present situation. Then decide on what you think is the most effective response.

The final step is to confront the situation and *respond* in the way you have decided is most appropriate. Maintain your self-control while you are responding to the situation. If you sense yourself losing your patience again, start back at the beginning and go through the four *R*s again: *Recognize, Remove yourself, Review, Respond.*

Try to move through the four *R*s as quickly as possible. If you take too long reviewing the situation, you may lose your chance to respond most effectively. When you remove yourself and review the situation, do not become caught up in all the details of the situation or all the possible ways of responding. After the situation has resolved, you can analyze it in greater detail and think about possible responses that you did not consider initially. Analyzing the situation later, when you are more relaxed, can lead to more creative ideas that might be helpful the next time you are confronted with a similar situation. At this time ask yourself, "What did I like about the way I handled that situation?" and, "What would I do differently next time?"

Managing the Stress in Your Life

Along with your thoughts about your child's behavior, other factors also influence your level of patience. Most of these are sources of stress. The more stressed you are, the less patient you will be. If you can reduce your stress or manage it more effectively, you will reduce the probability that you will lose your patience. A number of general strategies can help you manage the stress most adults experience.

Identify and Reduce Stressors

Unfortunately, we cannot eliminate many of the stressors in our lives. We must usually accept and work around stress factors such as health problems and job responsibilities. However, if you are like most people, there are probably numerous small stressors in your life that you can eliminate or reduce.

The first step is to identify what contributes to your stress. Make a list of all the stressors, big and small, that affect you. Then go through the list and mark the stressors that you can change or eliminate. For instance, some people become stressed by overcommitting themselves. If this is true for you, resolve to start being more assertive and reducing your commitments.

Other individuals are stressed by financial problems. If this applies to you, record all your expenses for one month and analyze exactly where you are spending your money. Many people who do this are quite surprised by the total amounts they are spending in certain areas. After you have clearly established where your money is going, decide where you can most easily make cutbacks and develop a budget.

Bear in mind that not only the "big" things, like finances, cause the most stress. For some people, the daily hassles of life collectively cause the most stress. If this is the case for you, try to plan your day to minimize the small hassles. Organization is the key. Try to plan out each day. For example, by developing a daily plan, you may be able to plan to do all your errands in one trip rather than two or three. This can be a big time saver and reduce stress.

In sum, the lives of most adults contain a number of potential stressors. The big stressors do not always have the major impact over time. Rather, the many small stressors, or daily hassles, often add up and lead to more ongoing difficulties than the major crises. The initial step is to identify the stressors you can change. The next step is to decide exactly what changes to make. Then do it!

Take a Break or Change Gears

If you were to list the most stressful occupations, you might list jobs like police officer, firefighter, or doctor. While these occupations are stressful, the people doing these jobs have time away from work to recuperate. They rarely work twenty-four hours a day, and if they do, they usually have periods of time off from work to recover.

Now, think about being a parent—especially the parent of a strong-willed child—and remember that the small stressors of life often have the biggest impact. This is especially true when we have little relief from these ongoing small stressors. From this perspective, being a parent of any child is one of the most stressful jobs in the world. We are parents twenty-four hours a day, seven days a week. Many parents of young children have little time off from the daily hassles of being a parent.

As the parent of a strong-willed child, you therefore need to take breaks from your parenting role. How you do this can vary greatly. Regardless of how you do it, the main goal should be for you to spend at least several hours a week doing something you really enjoy. Your activity might be something you consider relaxing, such as taking a nap, reading, going to a movie, or being with friends. Other kinds of breaks also can be helpful. For some people, just changing gears and doing something different from the routine of parenting is most helpful. For example, volunteer work outside the home is one way to change gears. The important point is to do something that you enjoy doing so that you can have a regular break or change of pace from the daily demands and hassles of parenting.

Learn How to Relax

When most people become really stressed, they show signs of physical tension. Common symptoms are tense muscles, headaches, rapid and shallow breathing, and increased blood pressure. One way of managing stress is learning how to relax in order to reduce such physical tension.

Many people believe they already know how to relax. However, effective relaxation is more than just sitting down in front of the television, taking a coffee break, or having a beer or glass of wine with friends. These activi-

Example of a Relaxation Exercise

The technique described here involves visualization and breathing exercises. This brief description alone cannot provide you with the skills necessary to achieve the level of relaxation necessary to significantly reduce your physical tension. However, we hope it will give you an idea of what relaxation training can involve. If you are interested in pursuing training in relaxation exercises, check with your bookstore for self-help books or audiotapes, or ask your physician or a local mental health association about the availability of such training in your community.

Before practicing this technique, lie down or sit in a comfortable chair that offers support for your head. Eliminate distractions by turning off the television and radio, taking the telephone off the hook, and choosing a location and time that you will not be disturbed.

Start by placing yourself in a comfortable position where all parts of your body, including your legs, arms, and head, are supported. Keep your legs uncrossed. Close your eyes. Try to focus initially on slowing down your breathing. Take deep, relaxing breaths. Focus on making your breathing smooth. That is, breathe in slowly and out slowly. Try to create a smooth rhythm to your breathing. Try to block out all other thoughts and concentrate solely on your breathing.

After your breathing becomes relaxed and rhythmic, imagine a small amount of tension in your body leaving through your breath each time you exhale. Imagine the tension being sucked out of your body each time you exhale. Imagine the tension leaving your feet, legs, back, shoulders, neck, and elsewhere in your body. Each time you inhale, imagine a small wave of relaxation spreading throughout your body from your head to your toes.

Try to continue this exercise for several minutes. Then daydream about a relaxing situation. For some people it might be lying on the beach, or for others lying in a field looking up at the clouds. The exact scene is unimportant as long as it is relaxing to you. (You should decide on the scene before beginning the relaxation exercise so you do not have to waste time and energy deciding on a scene when you are relaxed.) The most important thing to remember as you are daydreaming about your scene is to try to involve all your senses. Imagine that you are really there. Imagine not only the visual aspects of the scene, but also the sounds, smells, and sensations. For example, if you imagine yourself at the beach, imagine the sounds of the surf, the birds, and the children playing in the distance. Imagine the smells of salt water and perhaps suntan lotion. Also imagine the sensation of the sun's warmth on your skin and the feeling of the wind as it blows across your body. Try to actually put yourself at the beach mentally.

After you have practiced daydreaming for at least five to ten minutes, you can slowly open your eyes and focus on how relaxed you feel.

You can use such relaxation exercises as brief respites from the daily stressors in your life. They can be viewed as brief catnaps that relax and refresh your body. Over time, and with training, many people learn how to use such techniques to quickly put themselves in a relaxed state during times of tension.

ties may distract a person from stress or help the person cope, but they generally do not reduce physical tension.

One effective technique for combating physical tension is to learn and practice specific relaxation exercises (see box titled "Example of a Relaxation Exercise"). There are many types of relaxation exercises. Some involve learning to tense and relax specific muscle groups, while others involve breathing and visualization techniques. For these relaxation exercises to be most effective in reducing physical tension, you must practice them daily.

There are many ways to learn relaxation techniques. Mental health professionals often teach them individually. Your local hospital, community college, or other organization may offer classes in relaxation or stress management. Or you can learn on your own with one of the many books and audiotapes on the subject.

Learn Effective Problem-Solving Strategies

Problems in our lives, whether at work or at home, can be stressful. They can become extremely stressful when we do not know how we should handle them and, as a result, become overwhelmed. You are less likely to feel overwhelmed if you learn and practice a strategy for solving problems. One problem-solving process involves the following steps:

1. Try to relax and remain calm.
2. Clearly define the specific problem.
3. Generate a list of possible solutions.
4. Evaluate the solutions on the list.
5. Choose what you think is the best solution.
6. Implement the solution and evaluate the outcome.

To use this problem-solving process effectively, try to remain relaxed. The more tense and upset you become, the less clearly you will think and the less effectively you address the problem. When you are calm, clearly define the problem. Many times we do not effectively address problems because we look only at the symptoms instead of defining the exact problem. Once you have specifically defined the problem, generate a list of possible solutions. At this stage, do not think about whether each is a good or bad solution or even if it is realistic. You just want to brainstorm and come up with as many potential solutions as possible. Many people become so hung up on whether or not a possible solution will work that they do not allow themselves to freely brainstorm. As a result, they are less likely to think of unique and creative solutions.

After you have exhausted your thoughts on potential solutions, it is time to evaluate the solutions on your list. Review each potential solution and decide whether it is at all possible and whether it would produce the desired result. Also think about the negative repercussions of each solution. After evaluating all the possible solutions, choose the solution that you think is best, all factors considered. Some people never can make a decision because none of the options is ideal. If you are one of these people, remind yourself that most problems do not have an ideal solution (just as there are not ideal children!) and that you must choose the best possible solution for you. Typically, if you fail to select and implement a solution, you create more ongoing stress. Finally, at some point after implementing the solution you selected, evaluate the outcome and how you did in making the decision. Make sure you praise yourself if the solution you selected was a good one. If the selected solution was not a good one, use the experience as a time of learning. Think about other solutions that might have been more effective.

A problem-solving strategy that you can rely on not only is very useful to you, but also is a skill you can teach your child if he is at least six years old. Learning how to solve problems effectively is a very important life skill for children to develop. The most effective way of teaching your child such a skill is not through verbal explanations, but through your own demonstration of the skill. As we explained in Chapter 2, modeling is the best teacher. So try to let your child see how you go about managing and solving problems. Verbally walk your way through the problem-solving steps in your child's presence. Let him help generate some of the potential solutions. By your example, your child will learn to handle and solve problems.

Get Enough Rest

Everyone is tired at times, but frequently or constantly feeling tired is a problem. If you are like most people, you have less patience when you are tired. You may have difficulty seeing things objectively and using problem-solving skills. You may have a greater tendency to blow things out of proportion and to overreact to certain situations. Being tired creates problems that result in even more stress. If stress is a problem for you, you must get enough rest to effectively deal with the stressful situations you face.

Try to establish a consistent bedtime that will allow you to sleep sufficiently. Staying up past midnight every night and arising at 6:00 A.M. allows too little sleep time for most people. In the end you will be able to achieve more (especially in terms of quality) if you have enough rest than if you regularly stay up late to complete things. One way to do this is to have consistent times for going to bed and rising.

If you have difficulty falling asleep, you might want to try using the relaxation techniques discussed earlier in this chapter. Also, try to limit the use of your bed to sleeping. Avoid watching television, doing paperwork, eating, or reading in your bed. Do these other things in another room. In this way you will associate your bed with sleeping, which may decrease the amount of time it takes for you to fall asleep when you go to bed. Remember, if you sleep enough, you will feel rested, view things in a more positive light, and be a more effective problem solver.

While some people have difficulty sleeping when they are stressed, others tend to sleep more. If you are sleeping so much that sleep regularly interferes with your life, it is a problem, especially if you do not even feel rested after sleeping. If this applies to you, seek help from a professional. There are many explanations for such a problem that need to be evaluated.

Eat a Well-Balanced Diet

You have probably heard the expression "You are what you eat." You can argue the merits of this saying, but there is no denying that our diet influences our body's ability to function optimally. A balanced diet provides your body with the nutrition required to have the energy and health necessary to function well. A poor diet can result not only in a lack of energy, but also an inability for your body to fight off illness.

One of the major problems with stress and diet is that many people tend to eat less nutritiously when they are under stress. People under stress may eat irregularly and eat less nutritious food. Eating more "junk food" when under stress can establish a negative cycle. The more stressed you become, the poorer your eating habits; the poorer your eating habits, the less able your body is to help you deal with stress. So make an extra effort to eat balanced and nutritious meals, especially when you are under stress.

Exercise

Just as nutrition is important to our general well-being, so is physical fitness. The more physically fit you are, the greater your ability to handle the physical demands of stress. Unfortunately, when we are under stress, most of us are less, rather than more, physically active. The less physically active you are, the less physically fit you become, so the physical effects of stress will be greater.

Many people who regularly exercise or work out claim that it helps them manage stress. There is also growing scientific evidence that exercise provides benefits beyond general physical fitness. For example, endorphins (the body's "feel good" hormone) are released after a certain level of physical activity is reached. You should establish a regular exercise routine and stick to it, especially when your stress level increases.

Develop Support Systems

Don't try to do it alone! Life can be very difficult and stressful at times, and you need to be able to turn to others for support. This may mean having relationships with people you can talk to when life is stressful. Or it may mean building relationships with people who can offer more tangible support, like looking after your child occasionally so you can have a break. Remember the saying we mentioned in Chapter 11, "It takes a whole village to raise a child." Don't be afraid to reach out to others. Of course, an effective support system needs to go in both directions. Make sure you reciprocate by supporting those who help you, or your support system will collapse.

Maintain a Sense of Humor

When people are under stress, they tend to lose their sense of humor. They may fail to see any of the humor in what is going on in their life. This is unfortunate because humor can be a very effective way to manage stress. Laughing about things, and about ourselves, can really help us maintain a more realistic perspective about what is happening to us. Laughing also makes us feel good, and it can break tension. So try not to take yourself too seriously, and look for the humor in the situation. Sometimes laughter really can be the best medicine!

You need a big dose of humor when you have a strong-willed child. Such a child truly can test your patience. However, if you understand the role of your thoughts and change them when necessary, you are less likely to lose your patience. When you do lose your patience, minimize the negative effects by using the four *R*s: Recognize, Remove yourself, Review, and Respond. Finally, by evaluating and minimizing the stress in your life, you will increase your patience and make life more fun. The nine ways we recommend you manage stress are summarized in Table 13-1. Developing patience with a strong-willed child is not easy, but it can be done!

Managing the Stress in Your Life   TABLE 13-1

- Identify and reduce stressors.
- Take a break or change gears.
- Learn how to relax.
- Learn effective problem-solving strategies.
- Get enough rest.
- Eat a well-balanced diet.
- Exercise.
- Develop support systems.
- Maintain a sense of humor.

14

Building Positive Self-Esteem

Jim and Jon are five-year-old twins who live with their parents and infant sister. Their kindergarten teacher describes both boys as very popular students who are academically ahead of most of their classmates. Their teacher also believes they have above-average artistic and musical talent. The boys are average in terms of weight and height. Both boys are involved in a number of sports even though their athletic abilities are below average. The boys have a good relationship with their parents and sister. Their teacher and parents consider the boys attractive, popular, and gifted.

How do you think Jim and Jon would rate on self-esteem? Well, it may surprise you to know that Jim was found to have very positive self-esteem while Jon's self-esteem was well below average. How can this happen?

How Does Self-Esteem Develop?

Although self-esteem starts to develop at a very young age, let's first look at how it is established in school-aged children. Self-esteem in older children is based on both objective information that a child has about himself (for example, academic grades) and his subjective evaluation of that information. Objective information that may influence a child's self-esteem crosses various areas of functioning, including social, academic, and physical areas. Examples of objective information include how quickly he completes learning tasks, how many friends he has, how often friends ask to play with him, his size, and how fast he runs. The child then takes this objective information and evaluates it subjectively. Basically, he decides how his qualities and skills in a specific area stack up against what he thinks of as "good" for that area. As a result, a child can have positive self-esteem in some areas and not in others. For example, a child may have positive self-esteem in regard to his popularity and social skills and negative self-esteem in regard to his academic ability.

Although self-esteem can be broken down into different areas, when we refer to a child's self-esteem we generally mean the child's overall, or global, self-esteem. In other words, how does he feel generally about himself as a person? Global self-esteem depends on his self-esteem in each area and his belief about what areas are most important. A child's global self-esteem may be negative even if he views himself positively in most areas. In the example at the beginning of this chapter, the difference between Jon and Jim's self-esteem came from the level of importance each boy placed on different areas of functioning. Jon viewed physical and athletic ability as the most important personal quality and wanted to be known as a good athlete. Although he excelled in all other areas, his global self-esteem was negative because of his poor performance in the one area he valued the most. His brother, Jim, viewed popularity and academics as the most important personal qualities, and physical and athletic ability as secondary. As a result, Jim's overall self-esteem was very positive.

Understanding how self-esteem establishes itself in school-aged children shows what will be important in the future of your child. But how does self-esteem start to develop in the toddler years and beyond? As a first step, let's look at how children's perceptions of themselves change as they develop. Toddlers do not think about themselves in terms of abstract qualities such as friendships and popularity. They think of themselves in concrete and absolute terms such as "I have blond hair." Preschoolers also view themselves in absolute terms but start describing themselves more in terms of individual traits. For instance, they may tend to see themselves as either "good" or "bad." As they grow older and enter school, children start describing themselves frequently in terms of individual traits such as "nice," "messy," or "happy," but they also start to understand they can display different traits in different situations. They begin to realize that they are "messy" in some situations, such as when at home, and are "neat" in other situations, such as when they visit friends. As children develop through the early elementary school years, they also start comparing themselves to others because they are beginning to understand the perspectives of others. As they grow even older, children start describing themselves in terms of interpersonal traits (for example, shy or popular) and then eventually in terms of their attitudes, beliefs, and values.

Children also develop in terms of what they use as a measure for their sense of self-worth. For preschoolers, the most important areas include social approval (from parents and peers), cognitive competence (ability to learn and solve problems), and physical competence. In later childhood the important areas include athletic ability, appearance, academic performance, peer acceptance, and conduct.

In summary, self-esteem develops over time and as a function of the child's level of development. The two major factors that contribute to a child's level of self-esteem are his level of skill or competence in various areas (such as social, cognitive, and physical) and his relative evaluation of his competence in the areas he deems most important. Therefore, as a parent, you should strive to help your child develop the skills necessary to achieve to the best of his ability, focus on his strengths and minimize his weaknesses, and help him feel good about his strengths.

Why Is Positive Self-Esteem Important?

It is important to help your child build positive self-esteem. Children's self-esteem is related to numerous positive outcomes in life, including success in school, positive interpersonal relationships, and the ability to resist peer pressure. Children with positive self-esteem tend to be more successful in almost all areas of life than do children with low self-esteem.

Some people disagree, saying that positive self-esteem does not lead to things such as success in school but rather that success in school leads to higher self-esteem. In part, this is true. The relationship between self-esteem and success in life goes in both directions. So it is important for you to focus both on helping your child succeed by teaching him skills and on helping him view his level of ability positively.

Ways to Build Positive Self-Esteem

Developing positive self-esteem in strong-willed children is especially important. Many strong-willed children receive frequent negative feedback and relatively little positive feedback from others. Over time, this situation can start eroding a child's self-esteem. Therefore, it is important that you, as a parent, make an extra effort to build your child's positive self-esteem. Let's look at how you can do this.

Encourage Your Child's Interests and Abilities

We all have strengths and weaknesses, as well as different things in which we are interested. Children are no exception! While you should try to expose your child to many things and activities from an early age, you as a parent also need to develop an awareness of what things he is most interested in and of his strengths and weaknesses in these and other areas. As he grows older, continue to provide exposure to many things but strongly encourage the development of skills in areas where he shows a strong aptitude or ability. For some children this may be a certain sport, while for others it may be a special hobby or a skill such as art.

It is important to try to further develop the skills and interests in which your child shows particular promise. This will help him feel he is better than, or at least as good as, other children his age in at least one activity. This does not mean you should focus your child's activities in only one area, as he should be exposed to many different activities and areas. However, as your child grows older, his interests and special abilities will become more apparent. As this happens, encourage him to focus his time and effort in those areas.

Be careful to help him pursue *his* interests, as opposed to your interests. Do not try to fit a square peg into a round hole!

Offer Frequent Praise and Encouragement

All of us as parents want our children to feel good about themselves. One way we can achieve this is by frequently praising and encouraging them. If you think you already praise and encourage your child a lot, consider that in our experience, most parents think they praise and encourage their children much more than they actually do. They often think about their child in a positive sense without always communicating those thoughts very well.

Try to make a conscious effort every day to increase the number of times you praise and encourage your child. Table 14-1 suggests things you can say. Try not to use just one or two phrases repeatedly. Using many different expressions of praise and encouragement will be more

30 Ways to Praise and Encourage Your Child	**TABLE 14-1**

- That's great!
- You're doing such a great job!
- That's the way!
- Fantastic!
- All right!
- Outstanding!
- Nice going!
- You should be very proud of yourself!
- That's the way to do it!
- Wow!
- Good for you!
- You're getting better every day!
- I knew you could do it!
- You can do it!
- That's IT!
- You've just about got it!
- Terrific!
- You've figured it out!
- You're so good at that!
- Excellent!
- Good going!
- Way to go!
- Great!
- Super!
- You make it look easy!
- You're the best!
- Good work!
- I'm proud of you for trying so hard!
- I like the way you listen!
- Supercalafragilisticexpe-aladoecious! (from *Mary Poppins*)

effective. Also, do not focus exclusively on verbal praise. Offer a lot of physical expressions of praise such as high fives, pats on the back, ruffling hair, and hugs. Such non-verbal expressions can be especially powerful. Apply the principles you learned during week 2 of the five-week program, when you practiced praising and encouraging your strong-willed child (see Chapter 6).

Recognize Your Child's Normal Accomplishments

We all like to have our accomplishments recognized. Make sure you recognize your child's normal accomplishments instead of waiting until he does something outstanding. In addition to praise, think of other ways to further recognize his accomplishments. For example, post his artwork or other work from preschool or school on the refrigerator door. You might even consider having some of his best artwork framed and hung in your home. (This makes a great conversation piece when you have guests in your home!) Place other things he makes or builds in some prominent place in the house. If possible, take one of your child's masterpieces to your workplace so it will be on display if he visits you. Also, make a big deal about sending your child's work to other people such as grandparents or other relatives. Have your child make things to include in special-occasion gifts for family members and close friends.

By recognizing your child's normal accomplishments, you help him acknowledge his own abilities and encourage him to continue his efforts. This sense of accomplishment is strengthened by displaying his work and having others also recognize his accomplishments.

Encourage Your Child to Make Decisions

One of our goals as parents is to help our children develop self-discipline. By encouraging decision making from an early age, you can help your child develop not only self-discipline but also positive self-esteem. By making decisions, children develop a sense of self-control and accomplishment. As children make "good" decisions, over time they develop both a sense of ability and self-worth. If you as a parent make all the decisions for your young child, he will have more difficulty making decisions when he is older. The message he may hear is that he is not capable of making decisions or that you do not have confidence in his ability to make decisions. Furthermore, he will never have a chance to experience the feeling of success for good decisions and of failure for poor decisions. Both are important learning experiences!

We are not recommending that young children be made responsible for major decisions or the majority of the decisions in their life. However, children should be given the responsibility for making some decisions from a very early age. For example, during the early years, you can let your child choose which of two shirts he would like to wear. As in this example, limit the number of options from which to choose. It is best to encourage decisions such as "Would you like *this* or *this?*" Too many options can overwhelm a young child and frustrate you—especially when you have to wait an eternity for a decision! When he consistently does well selecting from two options, gradually give him more options from which to choose in making decisions. As your child grows older, allow him to make increasingly more decisions in a wider variety of areas of his life. In sum, children should learn how to make decisions from an early age, and as they grow older, their decision making should expand.

Let Your Child Take Some Risks

Parents naturally want to protect their children from failure. However, you do your child a disservice if you always protect him to the point of not allowing him to take risks that may lead to failure. Of course, you should not let your child take a lot of risks or engage in dangerous activities. At the same time, do not be afraid to let your child experience some failure. By taking some risks, your child will sometimes learn that he can do things he did not think he could. Successfully taking risks builds positive self-esteem. The key is for you to try to make sure most of the risks will end on a positive note.

Let's look at an example. Many parents would not let their three-year-old carry a breakable plate from the dinner table to the kitchen sink. However, if you think there is a good chance that your three-year-old can take the plate to the sink without dropping it, let him try. If he succeeds, praise him and let him know how much you appreciate him helping around the house. In this situation your child would experience success in something he had not done before and also would experience praise from you. As a result, he will feel more confident in his abilities and pleased with his contribution to helping around the house.

What would happen if he dropped the plate? Well, you would have known there was a risk of that happening and prepared yourself not to become upset. View the plate breaking as an accident and handle it matter-of-factly. This failure, like any other single event, is unlikely to have a major impact on self-esteem; only repeated failure damages self-esteem. That is why you want your child to succeed most of the time. However, learning how to handle failure also is important. If a child's parents never allow him to experience failure, he most likely will have a very difficult time later in life when his parents can no longer protect him from failure. Thus, try to view your child's failure as a chance to teach him how to cope with it. To make failure a learning experience, handle his failure matter-of-factly and praise him for his effort rather than the outcome. Soon after the failure, have him try a task at which he will probably succeed. Finally, let your child know that failure happens for a variety of reasons, not because he is a bad person.

In summary, the confidence from taking risks and succeeding in new tasks can really boost your child's self-esteem. At the same time, a little bit of failure early in life is not a bad thing, especially if parents help the child view minor failures as a chance to learn how to cope with failure.

Give Your Child Responsibilities

As we discussed in Chapter 11, children need to grow up believing that they make an important and meaningful contribution to their family. One way of achieving this is to give your child household responsibilities from an early age. In many families this might involve giving him specific chores that contribute to the family and home. For a young child, the initial goal is not to have him do some job to perfection but to help him develop a sense of accomplishment and contribution to the family.

You might have your young child dust the furniture in your living room. The goal is for him to feel good about helping, not do a perfect job of dusting. At first you will

Some Suggested Chores for Young Children

- Help set the dinner table. For very young children this might initially involve just placing a napkin on the table for each person.
- Put away toys.
- Help water plants.
- Help dust.
- Help vacuum. This could involve helping push the vacuum cleaner or picking up objects on the carpet, such as shoes, so that the parent can vacuum the carpet under the object.
- Place their dirty clothes in a certain location, such as a laundry basket or hamper.

probably need to offer a lot of encouragement and praise to help him to feel good about dusting and helping the family. Over time he should develop more willingness to do the job out of a sense of contributing to the family.

In many families parents wait until their child is older before introducing chores. Then they become upset because the child does not feel a sense of responsibility to participate in household chores. A sense of responsibility and desire to contribute to the family need to be cultivated from an early age.

Remember, with young children it is important not to pay too much attention to the end result. Initially, you may need to go back and redo your child's job. When this is necessary, do not let your child see you redo the job. If he does, the message he receives might well be that he cannot do the job to your satisfaction. This would decrease, not increase, his self-esteem. Remember, the initial focus for a young child is to help him develop a sense of wanting to help. As he grows older, you can focus more on how to do the job properly.

Don't Demand Perfection

Some parents believe that, when their child is not perfect, it reflects poorly on them as parents. If you tend to think this way, it is extremely important for you to come to grips with the fact that there is no perfect child, just as there is no perfect adult or perfect parent. All of us have our strengths and weaknesses. If you expect perfection of yourself, you are setting yourself up for failure. Likewise, if you expect your child to be perfect, you are going to be disappointed, and your child will learn that he can never quite measure up to your expectations. As a result, he will develop a sense of not being good enough to please you. Since most children want to please their parents, such a situation likely will lead him to develop low self-esteem. Also, putting too much pressure on your child to be perfect may backfire and result in his becoming resentful and rebellious.

Do not demand perfection. Instead, encourage your child's best effort. Remember that your child needs to know you accept him, flaws and all!

Avoid Absolutes in Describing Your Child

Try to resist the temptation to talk about your child in absolute terms, specifically when the terms have negative connotations. Avoid saying your child "always" does something wrong or "never" does something right. For example, do not say, "You are always so messy!" or, "You never have any respect for me." Parents usually make such absolute statements when they are upset about something their child has done. If you use absolute terms when talking to or about your child, he may start viewing himself as "messy," "disrespectful," or whatever label you have applied to him. If he believes you see him as always being a certain way, he may lose motivation to change.

Instead of using absolutes, focus on your child's behavior within a particular situation. Describe what you observe in that situation. Rather than saying, "You are always so messy," you could say, "You have really messed up your room this afternoon." This does not label your child as "messy."

Limit Negative Feedback

No one, child or adult, likes to be criticized. However, many parents make more negative statements than positive statements to their young children. This is especially true for parents with a strong-willed child. You may find yourself repeatedly saying things like, "No," "Don't do that," and, "Stop that."

Negative statements are sometimes necessary, but most parents provide too much negative feedback and not enough positive feedback. In some situations, parents may start off providing positive feedback, but the final result is negative. A good example is a back-handed compliment. This occurs when a parent starts by giving positive feedback but then turns it into negative feedback. A parent might say, "Jake, you did such a good job picking up your toys—why don't you do that all the time? Most of the time I have to remind you over and over to pick up your toys. If you would just pick them up right away, I wouldn't have to get mad and yell at you so much." What started off as very positive feedback will unfortunately be remembered as criticism and nagging. Back-handed compliments will have the opposite effect of what you desire.

Try to be mostly positive in the feedback you give to your child. For every instance of negative feedback you give him, try to give positive feedback three or four times. This will be a challenge, but it can enhance your child's self-esteem and help you see the positive aspects of his strong-willed behavior. Try to comment on your child's appropriate expressions of his determination, independence, assertiveness, and confidence.

Before moving on, let's look briefly at one other type of negative feedback, the word *no*. Many parents fall into a habit of saying no to our child's many minor requests. At times we sound like a continually occurring "no" recording. There is a saying we like that addresses the problem of routinely saying no to our children:

Say yes when you can and no when you must.

Don't Make Promises You Might Not Keep

When you repeatedly make and break promises to your child, he may believe that you do not care about or respect him enough to follow through with your promises. If this happens, he may start questioning his own self-worth. When a child starts questioning his worthiness, his self-esteem will suffer.

Keeping promises is also important for another reason: you want your child to view you as honest and true to your word. If you, as a parent, are honest and true to your word, your child will likely develop these traits. In the long run, such traits will help maintain his self-esteem.

The surest way to keep your promises is to think about what you are promising. Before you speak, ask yourself, "Will I be sure to follow through on this?" If you are not sure you will, do not make a promise.

Encourage Your Child to Use Positive Self-Talk

Try to encourage your child to say positive things about himself. When he does something good, teach him to say something positive such as, "I did a great job!" How do you teach your child to use such positive self-talk? As we explained in Chapter 2, one of the most effective teaching methods is modeling. To model positive self-talk, look for times during the day when you can compliment yourself out loud. These situations do not have to be the occasional times when you really excel, but whenever you do routine tasks well. For example, you might say, "I think this sandwich that I just made is great!" Then when you hear your child say something positive about himself, make sure you acknowledge it and express agreement with him. The more positive things your child says about himself, the more he will believe them and internalize the positive feelings about himself.

You also can encourage your child to use more positive self-talk by the way you provide positive feedback to him. For example, rather than saying, "I'm so proud of you for . . . ," you can rephrase the feedback to, "You should be so proud of yourself for. . . ." Such phrasing of positive feedback can help him internalize positive feelings about himself. Combine this type of feedback with feedback that expresses your feelings about your child. Ideally, you should provide a mixture of feedback that conveys the message of how you feel and how your child should feel about his accomplishments and behavior.

Teach Your Child Problem-Solving Skills

We all feel a sense of accomplishment when we are able to solve problems. Children also feel a sense of accomplishment and feel positive about themselves when they solve problems they face. These feelings accompany both major and minor achievements.

Try to avoid routinely solving all problems for your child. Instead, teach him to solve problems with as little guidance from you as possible. A good place to start teaching your older preschool-aged child how to solve problems is through play activities, such as building things with Lego blocks or Tinkertoys. Resist the temptation to build for him. Try to make statements that will lead him in the right direction or help him think of different possibilities. Let him discover the solution.

After you are able to help him solve problems in play situations, do the same in real-life situations. When a problem confronts your child, try to help him generate various possible solutions. After developing various possible solutions, have him evaluate the different possibilities and then decide on the best one. Make sure you use a lot of positive feedback as he works through the problem. Also, encourage positive self-statements when he arrives at his solution. These are the same steps we encouraged you to use in Chapter 13 to develop more patience.

As we noted earlier, the goal is not perfection. Young children cannot be expected to competently solve major problems, or even to solve simple problems every time. What is important is your teaching the process of how he can solve problems. The more confident he is in his ability to solve problems, the more positive his self-esteem will be.

Teach Your Child Social Skills

Children who have good social skills receive a lot of positive feedback from the adults and children with whom they interact. As a result, these children tend to have more positive self-esteem. While some children learn effective social skills relatively easily, other children have more difficulty. If your child seems to have difficulty interacting with others, you can teach him some basic social skills. However, it is important to remember that young children are not capable of very advanced social skills. When teaching your child social skills, keep in mind his level of development. For example, trying to teach a two-year-old how to play cooperatively with other two-year-olds will likely not be effective.

As with so many other skills, the most effective method of teaching social skills is through demonstration and positive feedback. Thus, if your child is two years old, you may have the simple goal of nonaggressive play. That is, in the presence of other children, your child will mainly be involved in his own play activities. Within this context, you want to praise him for short periods of time when he is involved in play rather than grabbing toys from other children or hitting them. Although you should not expect cooperative play, you certainly should praise sharing toys and other acts of cooperation.

If your child is four years old, he should be even more capable of playing around other children nonaggressively. This does not necessarily mean he will engage in a cooperative activity, such as building a tower with another child. However, he may share some Lego blocks as he and

Social Skills: What Can You Expect?

Young children go through different stages in their development of social and play skills. Although each child is unique, here are some general patterns:

- At age two, most children play by themselves even if other children are present.
- Between the ages of two and five, solitary play is gradually replaced by parallel play. Parallel play involves children playing in similar activities near each other but not with each other.
- Between the ages of five and seven, children engage in more cooperative play, which involves the give-and-take that we typically associate with children playing together.

Understanding your child's level of development will help you know when you should, and should not, try to teach specific social skills.

the other child each build separate towers. Your job as a parent is to praise nonaggressive play and sharing as well as to model how to share. As your child moves into the five- and six-year-old age range, include modeling of and praise for cooperative play.

Good social skills are an important way to build positive self-esteem. As a parent, you are in a position to teach your child skills that will help him make friends and feel good about himself.

Spend Quality Time with Your Child

Spending time with your child gives him the message that you care for and enjoy being with him. It is impossible to say just how much time a parent should ideally spend with her child. Different families have different constraints on time. However, you should try to spend as much time with your young child as possible within such constraints.

Even more important than the amount of time is the quality of the time you spend with your child. Spending hours watching television with your child is not high-quality time. Quality time involves having fun with your child and giving him your undivided attention. As we discussed in Chapter 11, having fun with your child is very important because it communicates that you like and value him. Such positive messages will enhance his self-esteem.

Be Accepting of Your Child

A major component of a loving and caring relationship is knowing that you are accepted in spite of all your flaws. Children need to feel that their parents love them regardless of their behavior. Continually communicate love and affection for your child. Let your child know you love him even though you might not like the way he behaves at times. This separation of a child's personal worth and his behavior is especially important for strong-willed children, as their behavior is often a source of difficulty.

In summary, we have presented a number of ways in which you can increase your strong-willed child's self-esteem:

- Encourage your child's interests and abilities.
- Offer frequent praise and support to your child.
- Recognize your child's normal accomplishments.
- Encourage your child to make decisions.
- Let your child take some risks.
- Give your child responsibilities.
- Don't demand that your child be perfect.
- Avoid absolutes in describing your child.
- Limit negative feedback to your child.
- Don't make promises to your child you might not keep.
- Teach and encourage your child to use positive self-talk.
- Teach your child problem-solving skills.
- Teach your child social skills.
- Spend quality time with your child.
- Be accepting of your child.

These techniques are based on the fact that your child's self-esteem is tied to his behavior and the reactions he receives to his behavior. Therefore, in addition to the strategies presented in this chapter, the techniques you learned in Part II for improving your child's behavior also will enhance his self-esteem.

In Part IV, we will present some common behavior problems of two- to six-year-old strong-willed children. Together, your positive home environment and the skills you learned in the Five-Week Program for Addressing Strong-Willed Behavior can help you manage these common problems. By reading the approaches to these common problems, you may also find ideas you can apply to any unique problems of your own child.

PART IV

Solving Some Common Behavior Problems: Additional Recommendations

At this point you should better understand your child's behavior (Part I), know the basic skills to address general behavior problems with your child's behavior (Part II), and understand the importance of a positive home environment (Part III). In this final part we discuss how to use the basic skills and other strategies to handle specific behavior problem areas for two- to six-year-old children.

15

Specific Problem Behaviors

Among common problem behaviors in two- to six-year-old children are temper tantrums, aggression, mealtime behavior problems, dressing problems, problems in the car, bedtime and sleep problems, lying, and sibling rivalry. We selected these specific behavior problem areas to focus on in Part IV because our surveys of parents indicated that they are of significant concern to many parents, especially parents of strong willed children. Before discussing our suggestions for dealing with these specific behavior problems, it is very important that you understand that the strategies we present in Part IV should be used only in combination with the skills and techniques you have learned in the earlier parts of the book. It is the combined use of all of these skills that will prove to be most effective in helping change the negative aspects of your strong-willed child's behavior.

Temper Tantrums

Temper tantrums are very common, especially for young strong-willed children. Tantrums can range from whining and crying to biting, kicking, throwing objects, and falling to the ground. Some children even hold their breath until they faint. When a tantrum occurs, it usually has a specific purpose. That is, temper tantrums are usually an attempt to gain attention, to get something, or to avoid something. No matter what the reason for the temper tantrum, you should communicate to your child that it is unacceptable.

If your child is prone to having frequent temper tantrums, remember that you will not be able to eliminate them altogether. All children have temper tantrums at some point. Your goal should be to decrease their frequency and their intensity. The following recommendations can help:

- Attend to and praise your child's appropriate behavior. This will reduce the probability of tantrums occurring. Especially use your attending and praising skills (from Part II) in situations that are frustrating to your child. Whenever he uses appropriate ways of dealing with frustration rather than having a tantrum, be sure to acknowledge it with praise and attention.
- Temper tantrums tend to occur more often when a child is hungry or tired. Try to make sure that your child has enough sleep and eats regularly.
- Look for a pattern in the timing of his temper tantrums. For example, do they occur mostly in the evening when your child is tired or before meals when he might be hungry? If you identify a pattern, you should try to rearrange his schedule to decrease the likelihood of tantrums.
- Intervene early, either before the temper tantrum starts or as soon as possible after it starts. Most children do not go from behaving appropriately to having a temper tantrum in a matter of seconds. More often, they first engage in inappropriate behavior such as talking back, crying, or yelling. In most cases, you probably know when a tantrum is about to occur. Whenever you have the gut feeling that IT is about to happen, intervene at that point—don't wait.

- Ignore temper tantrums. This is not easy, but it ensures that your child does not receive attention for his inappropriate behavior. Ignoring does not include leaving your child alone when this is potentially dangerous. Keep him in eyesight.
- When a temper tantrum occurs, make sure it does not work! Do not let your child avoid any responsibilities by having a temper tantrum. If your child has the temper tantrum because you said "no," do not change your mind.
- Try to relax and remain as calm as possible during your child's temper tantrum. Act as if you're in control and deal with the situation as matter-of-factly as possible. Never yell or give in to the temper tantrum.
- Acknowledge the fact that your child is upset—but only after he has settled down. For example, you could state, "I'm sorry that you were so angry, but having a temper tantrum is wrong." If your child is older than four, you also can ask him what would have been a better way of managing the situation that led to the temper tantrum.
- After your child's temper tantrum is over, move on. Put the episode behind you.
- Help your child learn to express himself with words. As children develop better language skills and the ability to express their feelings and desires, temper tantrums typically decrease.

Some children hold their breath during a temper tantrum in order to gain attention or their own way on an issue. Some children can actually turn blue in the face and pass out. When this happens, parents understandably become upset. However, breath holding is rarely serious and rarely has a medical cause. (But just in case, if your child holds his breath until passing out, it is important to have him examined by his physician.)

Most episodes of breath holding and passing out are brought on by frustration, anger, and attempts to gain attention. Therefore, it is very important that you pay minimal attention to your child if he holds his breath. This means not looking at him and may mean walking away. However, you should always remain in eyesight of your child. Try not to let your child know you are looking at him, but make sure that he is safe. If he does pass out, try to remember that children who hold their breath till they pass out typically start breathing again very shortly.

Aggression

Many young strong-willed children hit, push, bite, throw things, or destroy objects as a means of gaining their way or getting something they want. These types of aggression are most common in children two to three years old. As children grow older, physical aggression tends to decline. Unfortunately, verbal aggression often increases. Fortunately, there are some things parents can do to limit aggressive behavior:

- Attend to and praise your child when he uses behaviors other than aggression to deal with frustration and difficult situations.
- After the crisis has passed, try to teach your child alternatives to aggression. For two- to four-year-old children, you can offer them some alternatives. For instance, you can say, "When you feel angry, take a deep breath and come talk to me." For a child over four years old, encourage him to think of some ways of handling the situation other than by aggression. If he has difficulty coming up with ideas, you can suggest some appropriate ideas.
- Limit your child's viewing of television. As we discussed earlier, there is a high incidence of aggression in the media. This exposure comes from various sources, including cartoons, news shows, prime-time shows, movies, music videos, and video games.

- Limit your child's exposure to real acts of aggression. Try to prevent your child from being around aggressive children and adults.
- Make sure your child's aggressive behavior does not result in his gaining his way or being able to get something he desires. If he grabs or takes something from another child, he (or you) should return that object to the other child immediately.
- Try to remain calm and handle the aggressive episode as matter-of-factly as possible.
- Use immediate time-out for aggressive behavior. Do not give a warning for aggressive behavior. Giving a child a warning for aggressive behavior is like telling him that he always has one free punch before any punishment will occur.
- Acknowledge your child's feelings, but make sure he understands that aggression is not acceptable. For example, after you have dealt with the aggressive behavior, you can state, "I know you were angry, but you must not hit someone else—no matter how angry you are."

Mealtime Behavior Problems

Some young children are frequently up and down at the dinner table, throw food, grab food from the table, eat with their mouths open, or talk with their mouths full. Any one of these behaviors can be very frustrating to parents, especially when they occur continuously. When such mealtime behaviors occur constantly, parents often will respond by nagging and threatening their child. Such patterns lead to mealtimes that are unpleasant for both parents and child!

The most important step you can make toward improving your child's mealtime behavior is to make mealtimes more positive. Unfortunately, for many families dinner is a time when parents talk to each other about problems or what they did during the day. This makes mealtime very boring for children. In some families, children learn that the best way of gaining attention during mealtime is to do something inappropriate. To make mealtime more pleasant, have an interesting ritual that involves all family members. For example, have each person at the table talk about his day. For younger children with limited language skills, a parent can help tell about what the child did during the day. Try to focus on the positive things that happened, not the problems.

The following recommendations also can help you manage mealtime behavior problems:

- You and other family members must model good mealtime behaviors. Sometimes parents or older siblings chew with their mouths open or frequently leave the dinner table. It is hard to expect children to follow mealtime rules when their parents and older siblings do not follow them.
- Do not eat in front of the television. Mealtimes should be a time for families to interact. Sitting in front of the TV does not facilitate family interaction!
- Do not allow your child to have any toys or activity materials at the dinner table during mealtime.
- If your child misbehaves during mealtime, there should be an immediate consequence. For example, if he throws food, he should be placed in time-out. An easy way of implementing time-out at the dinner table is to pull your child's chair, with him sitting in it, away from the table. While he is away from the table, you should carry on a conversation but exclude your child from the conversation.
- As a general rule, if you use time-out three times with your child during a single meal, that meal is finished for him, and he should not receive any snacks until the next mealtime.

Table Manners

You can help your young child practice good table manners through play activities. For example, have tea parties or pretend meals with him. While playing you can talk about and demonstrate specific manners. Table manners that you can teach this way include asking for things to be passed by saying "please" and "thank you," chewing with a closed mouth, and asking to be excused from the table when the meal is over.

By the time your child is three or four years old, you should have some basic mealtime rules. These rules should be clear, specific, and within your child's ability. Examples include staying seated and keeping your mouth closed while chewing. Until your child is following these rules consistently, the rules should be mentioned in a pleasant way at the beginning of each meal. It is then critical that you acknowledge by praising and attending when the child is following the rules.

Picky Eaters

If your child is a picky eater, try giving him only small portions of food. You can always give him more. Do not offer dessert to your picky eater if he did not finish his meal. Also, eliminate snacks between meals if your child is not eating well during mealtime.

If he tends to stall and pick at his food during mealtime, set a reasonable time limit for the meal. At the end of the time, the meal is over, so remove your child's plate. Do not nag or constantly remind him to eat.

Restaurant Behavior

Many parents become frustrated when their child does not behave well in restaurants. However, if a child does not have good manners at home during mealtime, he is unlikely to be well behaved at a restaurant. Therefore, it is very important to focus on teaching your child good manners at home. Once your child is behaving well during mealtimes at home, start working on mealtime behavior in restaurants. Initially go to fast-food restaurants and then progress to family-style restaurants before taking your child to a "nice" restaurant where poor behavior could be more embarrassing.

Other things you can do to minimize behavior problems in restaurants include planning ahead and taking some toys or activity materials to the restaurant with you. Most children start misbehaving in restaurants when they're bored, especially when waiting for their food to arrive. Taking a special coloring book and crayons to restaurants can help keep a young child occupied until the meal arrives. Once the food arrives at your table, remove all toys and activity materials from the table until your child has finished his meal.

Before entering the restaurant, it is usually best to state your rules and what will happen if your child does not follow them. The consequences likely would include time-out. Try to decide ahead of time where you will have your child take a time-out if it becomes necessary. It might be in his chair pulled away from the table, in the corner, in the rest room, or in the car. Obviously, in the latter two places you would not leave your child alone.

As with meals at home, make sure to frequently praise and attend appropriate behavior and to involve your child in the conversation.

Dressing Problems

Many young strong-willed children resist getting dressed. This resistance might take the form of a child actively resisting his parent trying to dress him or the child's insisting on wearing an inappropriate type of clothing. Although we recommend giving children some choice in deciding what to wear, wearing a sweater in ninety-degree weather is not acceptable!

Also be aware of what your child is capable of doing in terms of dressing himself. By the age of two to three, most children show an interest in wanting to help dress themselves. However, by the age of three, most children can put on only large articles of clothing by themselves. By four years old, they can usually fasten large buttons. By five, they are typically able to dress themselves except for tying their shoelaces. Also, children can take clothes off before they can learn to put them on!

With these limitations in mind, here are some recommendations to follow for managing dressing problems:

- If deciding what to wear is a problem in the morning, lay out the clothes your child will wear the night before.
- Give your child some choice in what he wears—but not too much choice. It is typically best to let preschoolers choose between two articles of clothing. For example, ask, "Would you like to wear this red shirt or this blue one?"
- Allow plenty of time for your child to dress. In many households, mornings are frantic, with adults and children all dressing under time pressures. However, as you probably well know, it is very difficult to rush a young strong-willed child to get dressed. In many families the more you try to rush him, the more resistance he offers. Allowing enough time eliminates the "rush" factor.
- Make dressing fun. Sing songs to your young child. Play music on a cassette machine. Distract your child by having him look out the window or at a picture on the wall. Have your child name the colors of the clothes you are putting on him.
- Use frequent attending and praise during dressing. For example, say, "We are putting this sock over your foot, and we are pulling it up really high. Now we are putting the other sock over your toes, and up over your ankle, and pulling it up really high. Now we are slipping your pants over your feet, and we're pulling them up all the way up to the top."

- For children who leave home in the morning to go to a child-care center, preschool, or school program, it is important to establish a regular morning routine. For example, when your child awakens, he should brush his teeth, comb his hair, and then dress. He should not be allowed to watch television or play games until after he has dressed and eaten breakfast.
- If your child tends to stall and not dress in a reasonable amount of time, you can sometimes make morning routines more fun and effective by playing beat-the-clock. For a child who is at least four or five years old, set a kitchen timer for a reasonable amount of time to become fully dressed. If he beats the clock and is dressed before the buzzer goes off, he should be praised and perhaps offered some type of incentive, such as a sticker or the choice of a special breakfast item.

As your child reaches the age of four or five, he should be taking on more responsibility for dressing himself. To help him learn to dress himself, buy clothes that are easy for him to put on. Try to avoid clothes with small buttons or clasps. As your child is learning how to dress himself, make sure you praise him often. Initially, you can teach him to dress himself by taking the first steps in putting an article of clothing on him and then letting him complete the task. For instance, you might start by pulling his socks up to his ankle, then let him pull them up all the way. Or you could put his pants over his feet and have him pull them up. Offer a lot of praise and attending while teaching him to dress himself.

Behavior Problems in the Car

One of the most frustrating situations that parents face is misbehavior in the car. Since the parent is driving, she is limited in what she can do to manage behavior problems.

The primary recommendation for car travel is to make sure your child is always properly restrained. Correctly use a car seat, booster seat, or seat belt, depending on your child's size. From a very early age, establish that you do not start the car until everyone in the car, including yourself, is buckled in. Automobile accidents are the leading cause of death for children. The majority of these deaths could be prevented if children were properly restrained. Children who are correctly restrained are not only much safer but also much better behaved while in the car.

These other tactics can also help you prevent problem behavior in the car:

- Have certain activities that are "car activities." You might keep a bag of toys in the car for your child to use only in the car.
- Buy a cassette tape of music that your child likes. Play the tape only in the car and only when he is behaving appropriately. As soon as there is any inappropriate behavior, stop the tape until the inappropriate behavior has stopped.
- For long trips, take snacks and drinks, special games or songs, and picture books or old magazines for your child. To combat boredom, you also can play "I spy" with objects inside the car, counting games, or alphabet games.
- Frequently praise and attend in the car when your child is behaving well.

If your child does misbehave in the car, remain calm. Pull the car over to the side of the road and consider your child to be in time-out in his seat. That is, remain in the car, but totally ignore your child until he has settled down and becomes quiet. After he has been quiet for the length of time that you would normally expect in time-out, thank him for settling down, start the car up, and continue on your trip. When you're under time pressure, this can be very frustrating. However, your child needs to know that he cannot misbehave in the car. If your child often misbehaves in the car, allow extra time on trips in order to teach him to behave more appropriately while in the car.

This technique might not work if you are traveling somewhere that your child does not want to go. In this case it is best to continue on your trip. If he is under three or four years old, ignore him to the extent possible. If he is older than four, impose some loss of privilege. You also can use time-out after you have reached your destination; however, time-out is much less effective if it is delayed.

If you have more than one child in the car and they start fighting, stop the car and separate them to the extent possible. Depending on the children's age, you might have one child sit in the front seat and one in the backseat. If two parents are in the car, one parent and one child can be in the front and the other parent and child in the back. Separating children eliminates many problems.

Bedtime and Sleep Problems

Although bedtime and sleep difficulties have many variations, we are going to focus on three primary problems: resisting at bedtime, frequently getting up during the night, and having nightmares. These types of sleep problems are among the most common for young children. In many cases, they are much more of a problem for the parent than they are the child—especially if you are a parent who likes to sleep! When sleep problems occur nightly, the family can experience a significant amount of stress.

As you determine whether you have a problem and consider which recommendations apply to you, review the information in Table 15-1. This table summarizes the average sleep habits of young children. The times given in the table are averages, and individual sleep patterns vary substantially. Some children need less sleep than the average, while others need more than average.

Average Sleep Patterns of Young Children	TABLE 15-1

Age	Average Sleep Pattern
2	11½ hours at night plus a 1½-hour nap
3	11 hours at night plus a 1-hour nap
4–5	12 hours at night (no nap)
6–7	10–11 hours at night (no nap)

Problems Going to Bed

Putting a strong-willed child to bed is very frustrating for many parents. Some children refuse to go to bed, while others go to bed but then frequently call out for their parents or come out of their bedroom. All children sometimes resist going to bed or have difficulty falling asleep. This behavior becomes a problem when it occurs frequently.

Routines and Rituals

The basic way to prevent problems at bedtime is to make this a consistent and predictable time. Start by setting a consistent bedtime. Many children with bedtime problems have an inconsistent sleep schedule. It is hard for a child's body to establish a regular sleep/wake cycle unless his bedtime and morning waking time are fairly consistent. If your child goes to bed one night at 8:00, the next night at 11:00, and the following night at 9:00, he will have difficulty developing good sleep habits. Although no one is going to be totally consistent with bedtime, you should at least strive for consistency. Also, if your child is having difficulty sleeping, it is best to awaken him at approximately the same time every day, even on weekends.

Also develop a consistent bedtime ritual. This is a routine that your child goes through every night immediately before going to bed. It should involve about four to seven activities that are quieting and soothing, such as a bath, a snack, a bedtime story, goodnight kisses for everyone in the family, and arranging soft animals in his bed. This bedtime ritual should last between ten and twenty minutes. A longer ritual can be difficult to manage every night. If your child is having difficulty settling down at night, make sure the bedtime ritual activities occur in the same sequence every night.

Some parents find that using a beat-the-clock game can be helpful in dealing with their child's stalling during the bedtime routine. The parents set a timer for whatever time limit they believe to be reasonable to complete the bedtime routine without rushing. The purpose is not to have the child rush through the routine but rather to prevent stalling. If the child is in bed and has completed all of his routine activities appropriately before the buzzer or alarm goes off, he receives an extra bedtime story. If you use this approach, do not allow your child to have an extra story unless he does beat the clock.

Going to bed is a transition for children. Transitions can be difficult for strong-willed children. Therefore, tell your child about five to ten minutes beforehand that bedtime will occur in a few minutes. Try to make the transition to bed as smooth as possible. One way to do this is to plan for games and activities to end before bedtime. Once bedtime arrives, do not allow any stalling.

If your child has a habit of requesting a drink or expressing a need to go to the bathroom after the lights have been turned out, try to prepare to avoid these problems. Make sure your child has a drink of water before going to bed, or place a glass of water on his bedside table. Also make sure your child uses the bathroom before going to bed.

Praise and attend to your child during the bedtime routine. Attending to your child during bath, undressing, and other activities during the routine expresses your affection toward your child and acknowledges his efforts.

Make bedtime a loving time with your child. Avoid interruptions. For example, you typically should not answer the telephone during the bedtime routine, so the routine can be as consistent and calming as possible. Use this time to show a lot of physical affection toward your child and express your love. As your child grows older, you can talk about the good things that happened during the day and the good things that will happen the next day.

Difficulty Falling Asleep

If your child has a habit of lying in bed for one or two hours after bedtime before he falls asleep, it may help to temporarily move his bedtime to a later time. Move the bedtime to the approximate time he is naturally going to sleep. He probably will fall asleep faster because his body is used to going to sleep at that time. After he is going to sleep consistently at the later bedtime, gradually move the bedtime to an earlier, more appropriate time.

However, it is important not to move the bedtime back to the earlier time too quickly. If you're putting your child to bed at 8:00, but he is not falling asleep until 10:00, initially move his bedtime to approximately 10:00. After he is falling asleep quickly and consistently at 10:00, move his bedtime back to 9:45 for several nights, then move it back by fifteen minutes every few nights thereafter. Continue this procedure until his bedtime is back to the original time of 8:00. If you try to move the bedtime back too quickly, your efforts may fail because your child's body is not gradually adjusting to the earlier time of falling asleep.

If your child is still taking a nap, examine when this nap is occurring. If it is late in the afternoon, he may not be tired enough to fall asleep at his regular bedtime. Although we do not recommend eliminating a nap until a child is at least four years old, try to make his nap earlier in the afternoon and perhaps decrease the length of the nap.

If your child gets out of bed and comes out of his bedroom before going to sleep, immediately return him to his room. Do not talk to him or express anger. Rather, pick him up, carry him facing away from you so he cannot cuddle with you, and put him back in his bed. At that point make eye contact and firmly say, "You need to stay in your bedroom."

You cannot make your child fall asleep, but you can control what time he goes to bed and that he stays in his bedroom. The rule should be for your child to stay in his bedroom. Trying to insist that your child stay in his bed and go to sleep can lead to unnecessary conflict. If your child stays in his room but sleeps on the floor near the door, he will soon learn that the bed is the more comfortable place to sleep.

Another response if your child leaves his room before going to sleep is to close the door. If he is used to having his bedroom door open, you can leave it open initially when he goes to bed. Tell him that, if he comes out of his bedroom, you will put him back in the bed and close his door. Closing the door in this way is a method of enforcing the rule that your child stay in his room, not an effort to punish or scare him. If you close the door, have a night-light in your child's room so he will not be totally in the dark. Also check on your child regularly (as described later).

Fears and Anxieties

If your child expresses any fear or anxiety about going to bed, such as being afraid of monsters, it is important to address his concern. Remember, young children have very active imaginations and sometimes have difficulty separating fantasy from reality. You can use this to your advantage! Rather than saying there are no such things as monsters, say something such as, "My job as your mom is to make sure that no monsters come into our house." Another technique that has worked for many families is to buy some air freshener and cover the bottle with paper wrapping on which you've drawn a monster with an X through it and written "Monster Repellent." At night before your child goes to bed, you and he can spray the room to assure that no monsters will come into his room

Help Your Child Learn to Fall Asleep

If your child calls out for you, do not respond immediately. Wait at least three to five minutes before going to check on him. When you go, try not to pick up your child or to lie down next him in order to help him fall asleep. The problem for many children with sleep difficulties is that they are used to their parents helping them fall asleep. They learn to rely on their parents, not how to fall asleep easily on their own. Instead, go into his room to reassure him that you are still in the house and to reassure yourself that he is all right. Stay in the room no longer than one minute.

If he calls out again, wait five to seven minutes before going back. Continue this cycle, adding a couple of minutes each time before going in, until you are waiting a maximum of ten to fifteen minutes between checks. If you have temporarily moved your child's bedtime later, he will be that much more tired and should be falling asleep after a relatively short period of time.

This procedure can be very difficult for parents. In many cases their child may cry excessively. However, there is no evidence that this harms your child. Unfortunately, you cannot reason with your child about the need to go to sleep. This technique of waiting before going in to check on your child can take up to a week, but if you stick with it, it can be very effective. If you give in and pick your child up or let your child sleep with you, the problem can become more resistant to change in the future.

during the night. Of course, these techniques will be less effective as your child grows older. If he exhibits significant fear or anxiety about sleeping, you might want to consider seeking professional help.

If your child is concerned about separation from you at bedtime, let him know that you will check on him. You could tell your child, "If you are quiet, I will come check on you in five minutes." Also tell your child that he must stay in the room.

In many cultures children sleep with their parents during their early childhood. This is not the norm in our culture. However, if you want your child to sleep with you, then that is a decision that you need to make. There is evidence suggesting that, while some children naturally make the transition from sleeping in their parents' bed to sleeping in their own bed, many children have difficulty making the transition. We have seen several families where children in the preteen and early teen years still needed a parent to lie down beside them in order for them to sleep. We believe that, if your goal is to have your child sleep on his own, it is most effective to make it a habit early in life.

When your child is easily going to bed and falling asleep rapidly, it is important to praise him in the morning. You might initially want to offer a special item for breakfast or another small treat if he did well the previous night. Do not lecture or nag him if the night did not go well. Focus only on improvements.

Frequent Awakening

Most children wake up several times during the night but fall back asleep on their own. However, some children have a very difficult time going back to sleep. In most cases this is because they have developed poor sleeping habits from an early age. This occurs, at least in part, because parents have helped them go back to sleep, and they have not learned how to fall asleep on their own. The goal for these children is to help them learn how to fall asleep on their own. Teaching your child to go back to sleep on his own involves a technique like that for helping your child learn to fall asleep at bedtime. Also having a consist bedtime and a bedtime ritual can reduce problems in awakening during the night.

If your child is waking up frequently at night, it is important that you put him to bed while he is still awake. Do not help him fall asleep at bedtime. He must learn how to go to sleep on his own. Use the techniques described in the box titled "Help Your Child Learn to Fall Asleep."

If your child gets out of bed and comes into your bedroom, immediately tell him to go back to bed. If he does not go back to bed, pick him up from behind so that he is facing away from you and cannot hug you. Immediately take him back to bed and say firmly, "You need to stay in your bedroom." You may need to do this over and over again before your child eventually stays in his room. Your child must realize that you are not going to give in and let him sleep in your room.

The first night that you do this can be very tiring for you; therefore, make sure you do it on a night when you do not need to go to work the following day. Although the first several nights that you use this technique can be difficult, it can be effective. This technique works for a majority of parents within the first week and in many cases within the course of three to four nights. The first two nights are usually the worst.

Children's Nightmares and Night Terrors

Many young children experience occasional nightmares, particularly between the ages of three and six. Night mares take place during the lightest stage of sleep, so many children awaken during a nightmare. When this happens, they may be very frightened, since they have difficulty differentiating a nightmare from reality. To help minimize the frightening effects of nightmares, try these ideas:

- When your child screams out because of a nightmare (it is a scream you will recognize!), respond to him as quickly as possible. Reassure him that you will protect him and keep him safe.
- Be as calm as possible and use a soothing voice to reassure your child that he is safe and will be OK.
- Stay with your child until he is relaxed and ready to fall back to sleep or has gone to sleep.
- If your child is not fully awake when you go into his room and he appears to be having a nightmare, do not awaken him. Stay with him until he returns to a sound sleep or wakes up on his own.

- Avoid letting your child come into your bedroom and stay in your bed after a nightmare. This can quickly develop into a habit. It also can give your child the message that his bed is not a safe place.

Young children have difficulty understanding that nightmares are not real. Trying to say that the nightmare is "just a dream" is seldom very effective. Try to explain to your child what a dream is and that all people have them. Nightmares are normal, and the best thing you can do is to help your child cope with it by relaxing and falling back asleep.

Some children have what are called *night terrors*. These are very different from nightmares. While nightmares take place during light sleep, night terrors take place during the deepest stages of sleep. They typically occur during the first four hours after a child falls asleep. Although they are rare, they occur most often around the ages of four and five. If a child does have a night terror, he may have them frequently. Night terrors typically occur less often as a child grows older. The exact cause of night terrors is not known. However, they are not usually considered dangerous or of significant concern. During a night terror children appear to be very frightened. They may violently move around and appear to be terrified. Although their eyes may be wide open, they are typically still asleep. For this reason, when parents try to calm a child who is having a night terror, they often find that he does not recognize them or respond to them.

If your child is having night terrors, go to him as quickly as you can, try to comfort him as much as possible, and prevent him from hurting himself. If your child resists your comforting, do not try to force it on him. Stay by your child until the night terror is over and he is peacefully asleep. Try to remain calm! It may be even more frightening to your child if he does wake up during the night terror and you are upset. It also may help to turn on a light (not too bright) in your child's room. If he does wake up, he will recognize you and his room and be able to settle down more quickly.

Since night terrors occur more often when children are overtired, make sure your child has plenty of rest and sleep. If your child has frequent night terrors, discuss them with his physician to rule out physical problems and to consider treatment approaches. In some cases, medications have been used to treat this problem.

Lying

It is very common for young children to lie. This is because children of this age have not yet learned that lying is wrong. Part of the reason that preschoolers lie is that they think of people as either good or bad. They also think that it is impossible for a good person to do something bad. Thus, to remain "good" in your eyes, your child may lie. For most young children, lying is not done mischievously but to protect themselves from punishment or disapproval. Therefore, use initial episodes of lying as an opportunity to teach rather than to punish.

Young children typically tell two types of lies. The first type is one that you would probably consider a "tall tale." In these cases a child makes up a story that is not true, or he greatly exaggerates the truth. With younger children, these tall tales often result from their imagination and their inability to always know the difference between fantasy and reality. When your child is telling a tall tale, he is often expressing things that he wishes were true. When this occurs, it is usually best for you not to make a big deal about the tall tale, but to matter-of-factly inject some reality into your child's story.

The second type of lie that young children often tell is one to obtain something they want or to avoid something. When this occurs, teach your child that lying is wrong and that it is important to tell the truth. Here are some ways of doing this:

- Model truthfulness. Parents often lie! We frequently engage in what we call "little white lies," which we think are OK. A parent might lie about her child's age at an amusement park or at a movie theater, or she might falsely tell someone that she has a prior commitment and cannot attend a function. When your child overhears you telling these lies, it is difficult for him to see them as different from lies that he tells. Therefore, try to be aware of and eliminate your lying in front of your child.

- Praise truthfulness. Whenever your child is truthful about something he could have lied about, make sure that you praise him. Let him know you appreciate his truthfulness.

- Explain to your child why telling the truth is important. Start teaching your child the importance of telling the truth when he is very young. Also let him know that there are negative consequences for children who lie. In discussing lying, try to keep explanations as concrete as possible, and realize that children under the age of three or four are going to have difficulty comprehending the concept of lying. Give concrete examples of telling the truth and telling a lie.

- Try to remain calm when your child is not telling the truth.

- Do not let your child's lie work! If your child lied in order to get something, make sure that he does not get it.

- Try to be consistent in how you handle lying. Have a consistent rule about lying and how to handle it. As your child grows older and knows that he is lying, there should be some consequence for lying (time-out or the removal of some privilege).

- Avoid shaming your child for lying. It is fine for you to let your child know you are disappointed with him when he lies. However, make sure that he realizes what you are disappointed about is that he lied and that you are not questioning his worth as an individual. Avoid labeling your child as a "liar."

Sibling Rivalry

Sibling rivalry occurs in all families with more than one child. It is normal and, in fact, very adaptive for children. When your children are pestering each other, try to realize that they are learning valuable lessons about how to deal with and resolve conflict. Your goal as a parent should not be to eliminate sibling rivalry, but rather to minimize it. Sibling rivalry is usually strongest between same-sex siblings who are one to three years apart in age. We will examine two common times for sibling rivalry: following the birth of a new baby and as children grow older.

After the birth of a baby, many older siblings become jealous and may express some hostility toward their baby brother or sister. Other children may regress in their behavior. For example, if they have been toilet trained, they start wetting or soiling themselves after the birth of a baby. Other children may react by withdrawing or by engaging in more attention-seeking behavior, such as becoming more fussy and demanding of their parents' time. This is difficult for parents as they are trying to meet the new demands of the baby. Fortunately, when you are expecting another child, you can do some things to help your older child adapt to having a sibling and thus to minimize rivalry:

- Prepare your child for what to expect. Explain exactly what will happen when you are in the hospital and who will be taking care of him. Try to cover all of the details for your child so he will not be worried. Also explain what a new baby will be like. Tell him that babies cry a lot and they also sleep a lot. Let him know that, although you'll be spending a lot of time looking after the baby, you do not love him any less.
- Let your child accompany you to prenatal visits and listen to the baby's heartbeat.
- If possible, make any significant changes in the home several months before the baby arrives. If your child is

using a crib that you plan to use for the baby, move the crib out of your child's room several months before the baby arrives. Make a big deal about your child getting a big-boy's bed, rather than saying you are going to be using the crib for the baby. Also, if any room changes you plan to make will affect your child, make them well before your due date.

- Avoid asking your child if he wants a baby brother or sister. He has no choice in this matter! If he says no, you are really going to be stuck.
- It is usually best to wait to let your child know about your pregnancy until you are in the second trimester and the greatest risk of miscarriage has passed.
- Try not to talk too much about the baby being a play-mate for your older child. It will be a long time before an infant is able to play with his older brother or sister. Your older child may become disappointed when the baby is born and he cannot throw a ball or play other games right away.
- Try not to undertake new developmental tasks with your child, such as toilet training, around the time the baby is due. If your child is not toilet trained, either start toilet training several months before your baby is due or wait until several months after the birth of the baby.

You can use the following recommendations after the new baby is born:

- If possible, let your child see the baby in the hospital.
- Let your child help you with the baby. Try to make it a pleasant experience for all of you by using frequent attends and praises with your older child when he is helping. If he does not want to help, do not force him.
- Parents often make a big deal about taking baby photographs and having a baby book. Bring out your older child's baby book to show him and to have on display after the baby is born. You also can make a family photograph album or scrapbook for your older child to let him know that he is just as special as the baby.

- Make sure you spend time alone with your older child. As you know, having a baby in the home is very demanding. Your older child can easily feel ignored. Find time to spend with your older child doing enjoyable activities that you have done with him in the past.
- Do not ignore aggressive behavior. If your child is aggressive toward the baby, you must deal with this behavior immediately, using time-out. Of course, you also should praise your child for his positive behavior with the baby.

As children grow older, sibling rivalry continues to be a very normal part of a sibling relationship. Often it occurs because the children are competing for their parents' attention, fighting over ownership of something, or trying to be seen as superior to each other in some way. The following recommendations can help you minimize its negative effects:

- It is impossible to treat your children totally equally. However, you should try to communicate to them that you recognize their unique traits and acknowledge their individual accomplishments.
- Try to spend time alone with each of your children regularly. Try to have special, yet different, activities that you do with each child.
- Acknowledge when your children do get along, especially in difficult situations where they could easily fight with each other. Use your attending and praising skills.
- Avoid comparing your children with one another. Although each of your children has his strengths and weaknesses, it's very important that you not compare children with each other in regard to these strengths and weaknesses.
- Try to ignore minor conflict between your children. Let them work it out on their own. Intervene only if the conflict becomes physical or excessive.
- When your children are fighting, it is usually impossible to find out who started it. Unless you saw exactly

what happened and know that only one child was at fault, intervene with both children. In most cases both children contribute to a fight. Perhaps one hit first, but often the other child was teasing or provoking the first child. Do not try to talk about the fight when it is happening. First, put both children in time-out to give them a chance to calm down. The issue they were fighting about can be addressed later. Your immediate goal should be to separate the children and have them gain self-control. When you use time-out with two children at once, put them in separate time-out areas so they cannot continue fighting.

- After time-out, use the conflict as a chance to teach the children more appropriate problem-solving skills. Try to have them identify the problem and ways that they can deal with the problem more effectively in the future. Younger children may need some suggestions. As children grow older, encourage them to generate suggestions on their own.

- Try to ignore tattling. A child often will come to his parents to tattle on his sibling when he feels that it may get the sibling in trouble. When tattling occurs, tell your child to go back to his sibling and try to work on the issue with him. You can acknowledge your child's feelings by saying something like, "I know that must make you very angry." You also can ask your child, "What do you think would be a good way for you to deal with . . . ?" This type of problem-solving question will help your child think about how he can handle the issue.

Conclusions

We have provided some solutions to common problems experienced by parents of two- to six-year-old strong-willed children. Of course, a strong-willed child will display many other problems as well. But now you should be able to devise solutions to those problems by using the strategies proposed in this book.

Parenting, like any other activity, requires effort, planning, and problem solving. It is work, but it can be fun and rewarding.

Happy Parenting!

Words to Remember

A hundred years from now it will not matter what sort of house I lived in, what my bank account was, or the kind of car I drove, but the world may be different because I was important in the life of a child.

—author unknown

Index

About the Authors

Rex Forehand, Ph.D., is a Research Professor of Clinical Psychology and Director of the Institute for Behavioral Research at the University of Georgia. Dr. Forehand, a child clinical psychologist, has devoted over twenty years to studying behavior problems of children and developing strategies for parents to use to change those problems. Furthermore, his research has addressed the role of the broader family environment (such as conflict between parents, divorce, parental depression, physical illness) and its influence on parenting and child behavior. His research and applied clinical programs have been published in over three hundred professional journal articles and book chapters. His book *Helping the Noncompliant Child* (coauthored with Robert J. McMahon) has received national acclaim for its delineation of a proven clinical intervention program for therapists to use with parents of children with behavior problems. Dr. Forehand's clinical and research efforts have resulted in his recognition as one of the most frequently cited authors in psychology, identification as one of the leading child mental health professionals in the United States, frequent citations in the public media, and appointment to many editorial boards of professional journals. He has received the American Psychological Association's Award for Outstanding Contributions to Child Clinical Psychology, the Rivendell Foundation Award for Outstanding Contributions to Improving the Research and Delivery of Mental Health Services to Children and Adolescents, the William A. Owens, Jr. Award for Creative Research in Social and Behavioral Sciences, and the Creative Research Medal. Dr. Forehand is married and the father of two grown children.

Nicholas Long, Ph.D., is an Associate Professor of Pediatrics and Director of Pediatric Psychology at the University of Arkansas for Medical Sciences and Arkansas Children's Hospital. Dr. Long is also Director of the Harvey and Bernice Jones Center for Effective Parenting. Dr. Long is an extensively published scholar in the areas of family influences on child behavior and practical approaches to parenting. His research has been published in leading professional journals and books. Dr. Long has also been appointed to the editorial boards of many pediatric and psychology journals. A primary focus of his clinical and research efforts has been the development of strategies to help parents manage common behavior problems of young children. These strategies have included the development of various parenting classes and written materials for parents and pediatricians to use in managing common childhood behavior problems. In addition to his clinical and research activities, Dr. Long plays an active role in training pediatricians and psychologists in the science and art of parenting. Dr. Long is a noted public speaker whose parenting presentations are in high demand. He is a frequently requested speaker on parenting at the regional, national, and international level. Dr. Long is a recipient of the Rivendell Foundation Award for Outstanding Contributions to Improving the Research and Delivery of Mental Health Services to Children and Adolescents. He is married and the father of two young boys.